PROLOGUE

"Be the change you want to see in the world" Gandhi

This is a story about healing. About possibility and purpose. And while the first half may look more like a sequence of events that couldn't possibly happen to one person, the truth is it is about the possibilities of shifting towards a miracle minded-ness and manifesting peace and healing in oneself and others.

I am an international educator with over twenty-five years' experience working around the world. One difference between me and other international school educators is that I make the country I am working in my home. I do not see myself in a country merely to do a job, I dig beneath the surface of the cultures, lifestyles, and environments to uncover rich new learnings that have shaped me as a person and also put me into some difficult life-changing situations. I have been held hostage in a bank in Nairobi Kenya, adopted two amazing children from the same country, survived a train overturning in Thailand, been held under country arrest in Qatar for a crime I didn't commit. I have loved, and I have felt the excruciating

1

pain of that love, of course in that pain I have hurt others. At 43 years old, I was 7 months pregnant and was fired from my job in a country that I could not get out of and could not stay in! I have lived through the violent hands of the man I married. The hands that nearly strangled me to death in a small room in Nairobi. The hands that later manipulated the judicial system of my own country to have me convicted as the perpetrator of violence against him. What I have also lived through is the power of possibility when you choose not to be a victim. It is through this process that I have now become the founder of a sustainable educational development in Africa that is transforming landscapes in many parts of the world.

I was born and raised in Adelaide, South Australia and currently reside there after 25 years abroad. It had been my dream to sit under a mango tree in Africa and write a book of my experiences. However, I had never wanted the story to be governed by an egotistical process that made me something other than what I was. So, the story came to life in Africa both on paper and in real life. When I got to Rwanda, I found that mango tree in my garden and the experiences of my life materialized on paper.

Rwanda is a country that was devastated by genocide in 1994. More than a million people were brutally slaughtered in just 100 days. The growth, development and vision of its president and its people show that in life nothing is too great to overcome. As my relationship with Rwanda has developed and solidified, I believe that we have a lot of parallels in our realities. We have both been massacred and we have learned through sheer force and determination the capacity to heal when you understand with every cell of your being that it is possible to forgive the unforgivable and that in doing so you create the energetic foundations of healing for yourself and those around you. I truly

NOTHING IS TOO BIG

SUSAN KNAPP

This book is lovingly dedicated to Tashania, Aaliyah, Marley, and Amalia. You came into this world as my teachers and guides. While the road has been bumpy, I wouldn't change a thing. We have always been in this together and know that *Nothing Is Too Big!*

believe that it is only at this point that true prosperity and growth can occur for the greater good of humanity.

Rwanda and I have a strong energetic connection that I had never fully understood until I got back to Adelaide. Ever since I had watched Gorillas in The Mist when I was sixteen years old, I had always wanted to go there. During my early years in Kenya, I had tried many times, but the political volatility had made it impossible. Many years later on a dance floor in Qatar, I was approached by a tall man who wanted to dance with me. When I asked his name, I had not understood what he said, but I had clearly heard where he was from. That night I saved his number in my phone as Mr. Rwanda. In the months and years that followed this meeting, Mr. Rwanda would become the father of my child, the most abusive reflection of my inner wounds I had encountered in this lifetime, my travelling companion to Rwanda (where he had never lived but spoke the language fluently due to his upbringing in Kenya), Kenya, Malaysia, Qatar and eventually Australia. He was my greatest teacher because he was the catalyst that finally brought me to my knees with only two choices, live and raise my children or end it all then and there.

And while the book started its official formation under the mango tree in Rwanda, it, just like my life, took many twists and turns to finally reach its pinnacle. A large portion was organically written after I was fired from my job in Rwanda. Completely devastated and thinking I had done something antigovernment; I was terrified. Penniless, I sold my shoes to pay for bus tickets and travelled 39 hours on a bus with my two-year-old and Mr. Rwanda across central Africa to Kenya. Here I rented a room and bought a mattress. With Amalia in her travel cot, I sat on that mattress and began writing about all of

3

the experiences I had encountered over the last twenty-five years in the forms of letters to my mum.

We remained in Kenya long enough for me to find another job, which was in Malaysia and actually stay alive despite his drunken attempts for that not to be the case.

The job in Malaysia had me working and Mr. Rwanda staying at home to look after Amalia. As I was to learn the hard way, he would always say that he was extremely happy about this living arrangement, until we were actually in the thick of it and he would revert to his default process. I was reading Rising Strong by Brene Brown in between teaching English as a Second Language in a language center in Kuala Lumpur. Brene encourages vulnerability (and don't get me wrong, I love her work). What I didn't realize at the time that I started my practice of vulnerability was that it doesn't work on a narcissist. That healing came later and taught me that a narcissist will always use your vulnerability against you...and so the process continued. The emotional torment in Malaysia escalated. I would sob myself to sleep in the regular foetal position and wake up every morning feeling as though I had been hit by a bus. I would stagger through the days, applying mascara to the tears and face powder to the bags under my eyes. By the time I got home he would be nice again. We would go and eat out as is common in Malaysia and then the cycle would start again.

I solved this problem as I always did, by adhering to his wishes of moving to another country. This time it was to Australia, my country of birth, but where I felt I did not fit in and where I had not lived for twenty-five years. I applied for a visit visa for Mr. Rwanda, who was on cloud nine. Yes of course he was ok about having to stay at home and take care of Amalia, while I was at work in a small Catholic School in Far North Queensland. After all he would be in Australia. He was going to take care of me while I saved up the ten thousand dollars to pay for his visa and our life would develop as he had always promised it would. He would do anything for me and the children because he would be in Australia.

Within six months of living in Australia he had dragged me through a Far North Queensland court system where he had me convicted of domestic violence, for which as I write I am still on a five-year good behaviour bond for. I was in the process of officially applying for bankruptcy as a result of the happenings that had occurred when I finally managed to get out of Qatar. The bankruptcy completed in September of 2020. Within the first year of bringing him into Australia, he had managed to 'lose' his passport so he could not fulfill the requirements of his visit visa, which was that he would need to leave and re-enter every three months. His government refused to replace his passport as they had discovered the tactics, he had used to obtain it in the first place, and he was one hundred percent convinced (and told everyone he could find) that I had stolen it.

In September of 2017, my dad took ill in Adelaide. Mr. Rwanda refused to take care of the children so I could visit, as I could not afford to fly down with them. At the beginning of November 2017, I got a call saying my dad was about to die. I had just been paid and had enough money for a flight for Marley and I and we came to Adelaide. Dad died the following day. While his death was unexpected and terribly sad, I truly believe he opened a gateway for the children and I that actually saved our lives. By the end of 2017, the children and I had left Mr. Rwanda with the car, his women, and his lifestyle in Far North Queensland and we had moved back into my mum's house in Adelaide. Believing I was broken beyond repair, that move actually created the landscape for healing and trans-

5

forming not only my life, but the lives of my children, my friends, and our communities in Kenya and Rwanda.

Through all of my experiences I have learnt that nothing is too big. I have been very blessed to have received the insights from my life experiences that have led to my healing and the manifestation of an educational development in Africa that teaches children from low-income families.

So, I believe the essence of everything I have written can be summed up in this quote by Marianne Williamson...

"Our deepest fear is not that we are inadequate.

Our deepest fear is that we are powerful beyond measure.

We ask ourselves

Who am I to be brilliant, gorgeous, talented, fabulous?

Actually, who are you not to be?

We were born to make manifest the Glory of God that is written within us.

And as we let our own light shine, we unconsciously give other people permission to do the same..."

I would love it if you decided to dive into the pages of this book and experience my undying love of Africa, my children, education, and life itself and, if you know your light may not be shining to its fullest capacity right now, there is absolutely no experience, situation, man, woman, or anyone who we can ever hold responsible for that, for that responsibility lies within all of us.

PREFACE

This book was largely inspired by the work of Brene Brown. She speaks of the power of vulnerability and of fear and failure. She explains that it is possible to get yourself back up when you have hit rock bottom and that if a person is brave enough, often enough, then they will inevitably fall.

Hearing that line alone resonated with me. I had taken more risks than most. I had moved to Africa. I had adopted children and then had two of my own. I had married into a different culture. I had built businesses in Kenya and Qatar and bought properties that had left me completely bankrupt, both financially and emotionally. I had moved my entire adult life away from everything I had been raised to believe was the way that things should be done.

After reading Brene's book, I learned that sometimes we all need to accept failure at face value. I believe that failure is something that remains a cultural construct – i.e., an action that is seen as a failure in one context may be acceptable in another. So, whilst I had to come to terms with the idea that in some cases I had simply failed, I also had to question what failure was and really accept that I was doing the best I could with the resources that I had.

Brene uses the visual imagery of falling into the arena. In my mind, I often saw myself in a boxing ring, an umpire standing over me powerfully waving his fist as he counted to ten for me to be knocked out. I saw myself in that position over and over again during different periods of my life.

However, every time those images flashed through my head, every time that umpire was trying to count me as a knockout, he only ever got as far as nine. Sometimes not even that far. I always got back up and I always continued. And as I continued, I did so with new knowledge and understanding about myself and those around me.

Stories can be extremely powerful. They can perpetuate personal cycles of fear, self-doubt, and regret. However, opening ourselves up to our own vulnerabilities can also unshackle us from the pain of the past. Stories have the incredible power to help us rewrite our endings.

These letters encompass joy, fear, shame, failure and success and in writing them I have felt extremely vulnerable. They are my version of events and are told in the way that I have seen them and through my feelings and emotions. In telling these stories, I have taken ownership of my experiences and have explored boundaries, shame, blame, resentment, heartbreak, generosity, and forgiveness.

This is my story.

PART ONE
THE END OF THE BEGINNING

ON MY KNEES

December 2017...

"Maybe you are searching among the branches for what only appears in the roots." Rumi.

I stepped into the shower cubicle. As I reached to turn on the tap, a spider caught my attention. Its legs were the thinnest of thin - so fine, long and dainty. But what I discovered during the time it took me to shower was the enormous strength and power that those legs held. All that spider wanted to do was reach the top of the tiled area and be on its way. The water flowed over my body, and I watched the spider on its endeavour, curious to see what it would do.

I don't like spiders very much, and there was certainly no way that I was going to pick it up or remove it. Also, it was in no direct danger because the water was nowhere near.

So, I watched. I do a lot of my thinking in the shower and as such am prone to staying in for quite some time. This habit of mine was certainly not going to help the spider on its mission that particular morning!

The spider took a few steps forward and then stumbled backwards. Again, it attempted to climb the tiled wall, but just like before it slipped back. And so, it continued. A few steps forward and then a few steps back. Not once did it manage to take more than five steps forwards before tripping and stumbling.

As I watched this spider with its legs that appeared to be so fragile and delicate, I felt a surge of empathy for that little spider. That spider was just like me. My whole life had moved forward on legs that appeared to many as weak and not as purposeful as they should be. And then I would stumble backwards. I never stumbled as far as I stepped, although more often than not it felt as though the backwards motions outnumbered the forward moving ones. However, like the spider in the shower, though my legs may have appeared frail and vulnerable, in actual fact they were strong and powerful and there was never any other destination I would reach than the top.

I had conscious memories of being in a physical fetal position for the six years prior to meeting the spider in the shower. Subconsciously, I later realized that I had been energetically in that fetal position for a lot longer.

I remember being curled up in a ball on the floor, protecting myself from the physical and emotional blows that had become a part of my new normal. I had been crushed - physically, emotionally, spiritually, and financially.

By definition of the system, I now chose to live in, I was a bankrupt, single parent pensioner, who had been convicted by an Australian justice system that allowed itself to be manipulated by the one who had abused me. When he walked into that police station in Far North Queensland to file his claim of domestic violence against me, the policewoman asked him if he had ever been violent towards me. His response was, "Not in Australia!" Despite the fact that his statement had raised alarm bells to the police, I had been convicted in court and was currently on a five-year good behaviour bond as the perpetrator of domestic violence. This was against a six-foot two-inch African man who had been a semi professional boxer for the last twenty years.

I can't remember the number of times I would lie sobbing in my fetal position and he would simply step over me to get to the fridge. He would stretch to put his plate of food into the microwave, whilst I lay there paralyzed, often until morning when I would unroll myself, apply foundation to my face and eyes to make them appear a little less swollen and head into work.

The spider in the shower and I actually had a lot in common. Every day our goal was to reach a higher point than we had woken up to. All we wanted to do was stand on those legs of ours and climb.

On that morning in the shower, I could easily have channeled the water to spray the spider straight down the drain, never to be seen again. But something stopped me. Whilst I was completely and utterly broken at the point the spider and I crossed paths, I had not encountered one single event that had made me want to swirl down the drain and disappear into oblivion. And I wasn't starting now.

The spider and I were going up.

Both of us were twisting and turning through the navigational patterns of life, putting one foot in front of the other and balancing on legs that had carried weights never designed to be endured by a living creature. But somehow, we had done it! Our resilience had enabled us to reach the top of the shower recess.

I was born on the 12th of May 1970, in a small seaside hospital just outside of Adelaide, Australia. My parents had grown up in the same suburb and had attended the same primary school. As children, my younger brother and I loved looking at the photograph of both our parents making their first holy communion together aged about eight.

Years later, when my paternal grandfather was called by my maternal grandmother to come and repair something at her house, my parents met as young adults. My father had accompanied my grandfather on this trip and on that day reconnected with my mother.

At the age of twenty-one, my mother and father married on a cold August day, in a Catholic church in Adelaide. On their honeymoon cruise to Fiji, my father got seasick, and my mother got pregnant.

I can remember as a child of about ten sitting in the quadrangle at school eating my lunch. My friends and I would sit on the asphalt, our knees almost touching, squeezing vegemite worms through the holes in our salada biscuits and discussing our dreams.

My dream consisted of three very specific parts. The first was to travel to Africa, the second to braid my hair, the third to adopt an African baby girl.

As a family, our regular Easter holidays would usually involve camping or visiting the snow fields of Victoria. I remember having so much fun skiing and just being together. Visits to grandparents were always something we looked forward to. These were simple times that created lifelong memories.

This was the example that I wanted to set for my own children - to create memories that would last them a lifetime. This is something I believe I have achieved. The only difference is that their times have perhaps not been as simple as mine were.

As my university studies finished, I needed to decide what my next step would be.

One evening on the netball court, a teammate said she was heading overseas on a program that included Africa. As this continent had been a deeply embedded dream for me since childhood I didn't think twice. I was in.

So, I left Adelaide and headed to Africa as a supervisor on a teenage exchange program. This involved approximately thirty Australian teenagers billeted with families in Nairobi and Mombasa.

I had always been a real homebody. I rarely slept at the homes of other people and took solace in being in my own environment. Therefore, I briefly wondered how I would endure the torture of being away from home, but as the trip was only for three months, I believed I would cope.

Twenty-five years later, my journey has taken me to places I could never have dreamt of. Life has put me in situations I would never have thought possible. I have lived in Africa, Asia, and the Middle East. I have been married and divorced. I am a mother to four children - two who did not come from my womb, but are the most cherished children alive and two, who to the surprise of many, I actually gave birth to!

Now, after leaving Adelaide a quarter of a decade ago, it is time to tell my story.

My story of how I was held hostage in Kenya while bullets were flying all around us outside.

My story of how I was held under country arrest in Qatar, banned from leaving, prevented from working, jobless, homeless, and seven months pregnant.

My story of my four children and my move to Rwanda, a country I had always dreamed of.

My story of the people who loved me and the people whom I have loved. This book will tell of my return to Australia and the cruel betrayals I encountered by the man I had loved.

Most importantly I will tell you about the lessons I have learned through this journey of life and my belief that everything happens for a reason. I ran away from Adelaide, the country of my birth and my Catholic upbringing, desperate to escape the hypocrisy and guilt. But it was not until I returned to Adelaide after twenty-five years of searching among the branches that I became fully aware of my roots and the healing of my soul could begin.

The day the spider and I met, my soul was not just broken, it was shattered. This caused many people around me to believe I was beyond repair.

Meeting the spider in the shower at the height of my brokenness was like my awakening. In the presence of the spider, I no longer felt imprisoned by the fear I had embedded in my mind. The spider came as my teacher that day. It came to show me the healing power of life.

This is the story of how nothing was too big for me to fulfill my dreams. It is also the story of how different life experiences confronted me, how I dealt with them and how the resilience I often thought was lacking, was what made me even stronger.

The essence of this book is that we never heal alone. When we learn and work through the steps of forgiving the unforgivable in ourselves and others, only then do we consciously manifest and expand on our true purpose for being on this earth at this particular time.

DEATH AND GRATITUDE

November 2017...

"Let go of your mind and then be mindful. Close your ears and listen!" Rumi

I stood at the lectern looking out over the faces of about one hundred and fifty people, most sitting, some standing and some not managing to fit inside the room, but determined their presence be felt in this space on this day. I had not written a script, but in my head, I knew what I was going to say. I had received many emails from the organizers in the preceding week asking for my script and had replied stating I would not use one, but they should not worry.... the organizers had done this many times before and everyone had a script...they were a bit worried, but stopped emailing, perhaps knowing it would be what it would be.

The lectern was positioned about three stairs up on a stage. My children, their father, mum and my brother's family was seated in the front row. Next to me on the stage lay my dad. I could not see him as they had replaced the wooden lid on the casket. Next to the flowers on top sat dads favorite bronze statue of a skeleton (one from his collection of art deco bronze statues he had imported to see in his retirement). Pictures and memories created by his grandchildren and on an easel next to him stood an IKEA frame, the ones with all the individual photo frames meshed together. Inside each frame was an ink paw print of the dogs from the dog park with their name under their print. Their owners were in the audience celebrating my dad's life.

As silver beams shone through the skylights at Centennial Park in Adelaide, I stood at that lectern without a script, dad in a wooden box next to me and I began to eulogize my father.

"All of you know I am a teacher and as such spend a lot of time telling stories. Inside those stories are many characters. The story has a plot and a setting and today we are at the end of that chapter with Ron's physical life with us. Together we have formed the story of his life and he has formed that in ours. I would like you to all open your palm. With the thumb of your opposite hand, I would like you to push into your palm and wrap your fingers around the thumb. If you can hold yourself there until I have finished, you will see where this story is going." Truth be told, having my own thumb pressed inside the palm of my opposite hand, thumb nail pressing in to create the physical pain which lessened the emotional pain, helped me not to lose control of my emotions.

I continued with some stories and many thankyous to the characters in this story. At the end there was meant to be a photo of dad sitting proudly in his regular striped polo shirt, arms folded across his chest and beer on the table. As the funeral director accidently forgot to put it up, I asked the guests to hold their enclosed hand towards the box where dad lay. I asked them to think of one thing they were grateful for about my dad, to breathe into that feeling and then together we all released that gratitude, and it was sent off to heaven with my dad.

As I worked through the grief of my dad not being around and through my daily yoga practice, I came to the belief that dad had died to save my life and the lives of my children. His physical departure opened a gateway for the children and I to leave the slow death of a domestically abusive relationship that over the preceding year (my first one back in Australia in twenty years) had left us physically, emotionally, spiritually, and financially bankrupt. In Dad's death I saw life. His grandchildren and I were able to now be housed in the family home, where we were physically safe and where I was in a position to heal and rebuild.

I was so grateful to be able to recognize dad's departure from the physical world as a miracle of life. Our relationship grew stronger, just in a different form and the lessons I have learned changed all of our lives.

BEGINNINGS

"Trust in dreams, for in them is the hidden gate to eternity. When you reach the end of what you should know you will be at the beginning of what you should sense." Khalil Gibran

Dear Mum

Growing up, we were always so close. The strength you gave our family, along with your wisdom and generous spirit, was something that has enriched all our lives in ways that you will never know. As a child I hated leaving you. Sleep over's were not an activity I would partake in. I just couldn't bear to be away from you. Then, as my university studies finished, my life took a path that as a child I could never have imagined.

At 45 years old, as I sat under a mango tree in Rwanda, I could not help but wish you were here. How I would have loved to share a cup of coffee with you and talk about the life experiences we have had whilst apart. But because you were not there, I decided to write them down and tell you the things I would have told you in our everyday chatter. These are the stories that you would have experienced had we been together; but they are also stories that would not have existed had I not left Adelaide and explored the world in the manner that I did.

So, as you know, when I finished University, I left Adelaide. This was only meant to be for three months, but now it is twenty-five years later. My journey has taken me to amazing places and put me in positions I would never have thought possible.

Your little girl from Adelaide has seen and done many things. She has laughed and cried, but never once has she not wished you were by her side to experience the joys and the heartaches together.

Now it is time to tell you my story.

Love always Susan

ONE WAY TICKET

31st December 2014, Doha, Qatar

"If life were predictable it would cease to be life and be without
flavour" Elenore Roosevelt.

Dear Mum

Today I put my three children on an airplane alone, for them to
make a sixteen-hour journey to Australia. I cannot even begin
to tell you the point of desperation I had reached to be in a position to even contemplate sending my children away. They are
so young. Marley, five and Aaliyah ten. Luckily, my pride and
joy, Tashania at seventeen was such a seasoned traveler that I
knew she would be able to handle her little brother and sister
on such a journey. Even with a change of flight in Abu Dhabi.

This morning, we woke up early and went to the Corniche in
Doha. We took an old Arab sailing ship for a ride around
the bay.

Being December, the weather was amazing. We enjoyed the scenery and laughed a lot. But the pain in my heart was indescribable. We took lots of photographs and after the ride we enjoyed breakfast together.

Eventually as evening fell, we headed for the airport. I was so worried that little Marley would not want to leave me. He was such a character, and his unpredictable behaviour could be challenging at times.

I checked them in. The airline attendant asked if I was sure they would be OK on such a long journey without an adult. I replied that they would be fine. As I looked at them, each clutching their hand luggage, ticket and passport, tears streamed down my face. My sweet Marley looked at me and said "Mummy, why are you crying so much?" Of course, that made it even worse! My little guy who I thought would struggle most with the departure, hugged me, waved goodbye, picked up his bag and carrying his own passport proceeded through immigration with his sisters.

It was at that point that my knees collapsed from under me. What mother does this to her children? I could barely move and needed to be escorted to the car and driven home. My only reassurance was that this time apart would only be for a month or two - little did I know at the time that was not to be the case.

With my children safely in Australia, I focused on my mission which was to get myself and my youngest daughter, Amalia out of Qatar. The twisted scenario that had engulfed our lives in this Middle Eastern country had sunk me to what I thought was rock bottom.

However, as time passed, it became clear that rock bottom is something that is time and place specific. Looking back, the fact that the children were in Australia was certainly an advantage. As the following year went on, I came to realize that nothing was more important than them being in the safety of the environment in Australia.

Love Susan

DEVASTATION

August 2015, Kigali, Rwanda

"The weird, weird thing about devastating loss is that life
actually does go on. When you're faced with a tragedy, a loss so
huge that you have no idea how you can live through it,
somehow the world keeps turning. The seconds keep ticking."
James Patterson

Dear Mum.

Devastation was not an emotion I was familiar with, until the
day I received an email from Australia telling me that my children would not be coming to live with me in Rwanda after all.
This was the first time in my life that I felt truly powerless.

When I opened the email on that wretched day and read such
agonizing news, I was not to know that this day would in fact
prove to be one filled with a new life perspective. A perspective
on what it really meant to lose a child.

I had always planned to come back to Australia and collect the children. Now that I had settled in Rwanda, with a nice house, comfortable lifestyle and good job, the time had come for me to return for my children.

Then, out of the blue, the email arrived from their father, telling me that he did not want the children to come. I was utterly heartbroken. It is hard to put into words the complete anguish I felt when I received this news. My head spun and I didn't know what to think or do.

Immediately after receiving that email, I had to attend a meeting with my boss. In our conversation, he started telling me different stories about members of the staff, most of whom were Rwandan. In Rwanda there are two categories of people. Before 1994, the categories were called Hutus and Tutsis. After 1994, these categories became known as the Diaspora and the Survivors. A Survivor is someone who lived in Rwanda during the genocide of 1994 and lived.

The teacher my boss told me about was a Survivor. She had been inside her house when the militia had barged in. They massacred her children, right in front of her eyes. In the commotion, one of her daughters managed to escape. After the genocide ended, this colleague of mine spent one-year walking around the country trying to find her child. She never succeeded.

This was a wakeup call. I was wallowing in my own self-pity, believing that I had lost my children, when in actual fact they were safe and well and being taken care of by a parent who loved them just as much as I did. This colleague of mine would have given anything to have that knowledge of her own children.

Therefore, I made peace with the fact that my children were in the place where they were meant to be and doing what they were meant to be doing. They were going to school, playing Aussie rules football and getting to spend valuable time with their father.

This led to reflections on the whole experience and of all the women working in Qatar and other Middle Eastern countries, who regularly leave their children so that they can earn money for them to eat and go to school. These women don't see their children for years and often miss their entire childhood in the quest for money.

I, on the other hand, knew that when the timing was right my children would return.

As I write this letter, the children have now been away from me for almost a year. It has been one of the toughest challenges I have ever had to deal with. A dear friend once said to me that the greatest gift we can give our children is the gift of letting them go. A tough lesson to learn, but I have certainly learned the truth in it.

Love Susan

ANOTHER KNOCKOUT

November 2013-February 2015, Al Khor, Qatar

"If you set your goals ridiculously high and it's a failure, you will fail above everyone else's success." James Cameron

Dear Mum

Qatar had been a country that we as a family had stumbled upon almost by accident. We were looking for a country that would offer two working visas to ex-patriots who were not both teachers. In addition, we were looking for an employment package that would provide us with free education for the children and a salary that would give us a good standard of living. We quickly discovered that Qatar could offer this and a lot more.

When I moved to Qatar, I only had one child. Tashania was seven years old and was to enter year 3 at the school I would be working in. In the ten years I was to stay in Qatar three more children would come into my life, but those are stories for another letter. This one is about the final months.

At seven months pregnant with my second biological child but fourth child in my family, a lady came into my office. She was holding small pieces of paper that had been sloppily stapled together and had various names handwritten in lead pencil across the top. She didn't even know who she was looking for, as she was new and the school was big,

I opened the letter which read that I should be present in the headmaster's office at a particular time to discuss HR matters. My heart sank. I was about to have a baby. My children went to school based on this job. We were housed because of this job. We had visas to remain in the country because of this job. I had a bank loan that was based on the job and had two years remaining before it would be complete. And I knew what the HR matters were going to be!

Twenty-five other people had been given the same slip of paper on the day that I was given. Some had entered the headmaster's office before me and all of them came out knowing that they had been fired. For me, with my heavy stomach and being heavily committed to the job, I could barely stand, and a friend had to enter with me. I sat down and was told my contract was being terminated. The following day Tashania was to leave for her International Award Gold Expedition in Nepal. She was to enter her final year of school the following academic year and now everything had been turned upside down. I looked at the headmaster and told him the opportunities he had single-handedly ruined for my children and then I walked out of the office. I got to the parking and collapsed. What on earth was I going to do?

After crying for hours, I decided that I needed to get a systematic approach to dealing with this problem. It was December. The baby was due in March, and I was still employed until July, so I did have a bit of time to prepare.

Qatar has some very unique labor laws. It is uncommon for an employee to be able to change employment whilst in Qatar, unless they either get a letter of no objection from their current sponsor, or they leave the country for a period of two years. After this they are entitled to switch to another job. Qatar also has very strict laws on employing women as the main sponsor. In order to live in Qatar, you must have a work visa and all family members are then sponsored by the main visa holder. In most cases, as this is a male-dominated society, the main sponsor is the husband. Of course, for me that was not the case.

Luckily, I had a letter of no objection from my company, meaning I could change to another job. The new problem that arose was that I had been on a very high-level employment package and there were no other schools in the country that could match it. The biggest issue was free education for the children. Education in Qatar is very expensive and on a teacher's salary, I would not have been able to afford having tuition deducted.

Step one in the plan, was to have the baby. I had decided to try a natural birth as I had really suffered with the caesarean with Marley and didn't want to go through that again. After Amalia was born and I had recovered from another caesarean, I really needed to start working on step two of the plan.

After numerous interviews within Qatar, the end of June was fast approaching, and I still had no job that would accommodate my children's education. I was now also facing a new challenge which was the fact that my visa was about to expire.

Visa regulations in Qatar are directly linked to your employer. Therefore, because I no longer had an employer who would renew my visa, I was about to hold an illegal visa status. As I was the sponsor of the children, I quickly paid a visit to immigration and got their visas extended for another year before mine expired. Thus at least three out of the five of us were legal. Amalia's visa status will come later in this story.

The end of June came, and my final settlement was put into my bank account. This along with the money for my air tickets and my gratuity amounted to quite a sizable sum. However, the minute it was deposited, the account was frozen, I had a travel ban imposed on me, meaning I was forbidden to leave the country and I was banned from selling my car. This was because the amount outstanding on the loan was still in excess of the amount deposited. In addition, I now had a court case, the outcome of which would determine my fate in the State of Qatar.

One of the challenges of living in Qatar is the fact that government departments all function in Arabic. Thus, the male dominated court had all written communication in Arabic and needless to say all verbal communication in Arabic. In fact, the signs on the courthouse are also in Arabic, as are the buttons on the lift inside the building.

I stumbled upon my court date after spending an hour traipsing through the building trying to find out what I was meant to do. I had not had any communication from the courts so knew I had to take matters into my own hands. I was given the date and told I needed to prepare a statement of events and have it translated into Arabic and present it to the court on that day. I had also been advised to attend court with my children.

It was now almost two months after I had finished work. I was still living in my company housing, although they were trying very hard to evict me. I had nowhere to go and four children, including a newborn baby.

With four children in tow, I dressed in my beautiful abaya, as a sign of respect for the court hearing and off we went to the courthouse. As we entered the room Marley was suddenly very hungry and proceeded to open the snacks, we had prepared for him. The entire courthouse was in shock. Tall Arab men dressed in suits or their pristine traditional thobes looked at us in disbelief. We were quickly escorted out into a private room and told to wait until we were called. After about an hour, I was called to stand in front of the judge. In my mind the only logical outcome was that I would need to be reinstated to my job in order to pay the loan, or the loan would have to be dissolved and I would be free to leave Qatar. Unfortunately for me, neither of these choices were the outcome.

It is important to note in this entire scenario that I had not even committed a crime. The money that was frozen inside my account was being used to pay the monthly installments of the loan, therefore I had not even defaulted one payment. Despite that I still had this entire court case swimming around me.

The judge declared that I would need to come back at another date about one month away in order to hear the verdict. One more month. Where would I live? What would happen to my children? How would we survive in this country without an income?

We were now at the point of absolute eviction. At the last minute, I managed to find myself a teaching job and even though I would be working under an illegal status, the job was providing us with a house and school fees for the children. I therefore started working and things moved on.

My next court date came, and I discovered that this was a situation that was not going to go away in a hurry. I met some representatives from the bank who told me that they file around twenty cases like mine every day. That was one hundred cases a week! Additionally, people across the country had been held under this situation of country arrest for years. I was now really starting to panic. That just couldn't happen to me.

In the middle of this entire scenario was the legal status of my newborn. Despite the fact that she had been born in Qatar, she was not Qatari and at the time had no legal status to enable her to remain in Qatar. In order for her to have obtained sponsorship by me, I needed a letter of permission from my company stating that they had no objection to the baby having residency in Qatar. At the initial point of being fired from my job I had asked the Human Resource Manager if they would still issue me with that letter despite the fact that they were firing me. She had verbally assured me that they would follow through with that commitment. They did not! I was therefore between a rock and a hard place. Luckily the other three children did have legal status and were in a position to leave Qatar if the situation got so bad that that was going to be our only option.

So, Amalia remained illegal. I continued to work illegally, until I got called into the office and was told by my boss that I did not fit in with their school and that my employment would cease in December. Now my options were diminishing quickly. I would not get another job at this time of year. We were going to lose our house again, along with the right of the children to go to school. There was no other option. The children would have to be sent to Australia to stay with their father until this mess was sorted out. And so, came the 30th of December and they left.

Friends are amazing people and the strength that I gained from the goodwill of others was truly amazing. A dear friend allowed Amalia and I to move into her house for as long as we needed. Others had also offered, but hers was the most practical.

Within one year, I had been fired from my job, had a baby, been evicted from my house...twice, had my children lose their right to school ...twice, stared a court case in an Arab country, for a crime that had not yet been committed and now I was about to lose my children.

As the court case continued there was no end in sight. It seems this is normal practice in Qatar and the judicial system does not see it as unusual. Meanwhile, I was spiralling into more of a cycle of depression. There was no logic behind what I was experiencing. I had lost my job without choice. There was no record of misconduct and no justification for the mass sackings that had occurred, as they had replaced all the people they had terminated.

On the day I got fired from my illegal job, I checked online to see if there was anything good happening job wise outside of Qatar. I knew nothing was going to happen inside. I found my dream job advertised in Rwanda. I had always wanted to go to Rwanda. Amalia's father was half Rwandan, and the job was perfect for my qualifications. I applied and the same day got a call from the school's Director saying they would interview me for the position the following day. My head was spinning. Had all this happened in Qatar to take me to Rwanda? When I was fired from my illegal job, I responded to the two people firing me with a comment that said, I know I am meant to be running my own school in Africa. Now Africa was calling me.

So, I had the interview. The hour-long conversation began with the line that the current Vice Principal had worked with me twenty years ago in Kenya and ended up with the Director of school telling me he would be in Qatar at the end of January. In my head I thought....'this job is mine!'

As my court case continued in Qatar, still with no end in sight, I felt there was no other option but to call you and dad and rack your brains for a solution.

How could I possibly expect you to understand the absurdity of what was happening to me in Qatar? Even people who lived with me in Qatar were having difficulty comprehending what was happening. For people so far away and with such a different sense of banking and a court system, understanding was certainly a tall order.

Your solution however completely bailed me out of a no-win situation and although I was so ashamed of having to take money from you at my age and having had the life I had in Qatar, the loan was paid, and the court case was dropped. I was now free to leave Qatar...but Amalia was not!

I got a call saying I had been offered the job in Rwanda. With the loan paid, my travel ban was lifted, and I was now free to leave Qatar. Amalia however was still under an illegal visa status and was not permitted to leave the country. The next step of my departure was a newly formed relationship with the immigration authorities of Qatar.

The first step that the immigration officials did not understand was why my company had refused to issue me with the letter of authorization for Amalia to get a visa when she was born. Of course, I did not have an answer to such a logical question.

After numerous visits to immigration and having gained an understanding of many of the offices and procedures inside this building, the very helpful officer issued Amalia with a tourist visa. With this visa she would be in a position to leave the country of her birth! We were almost there! Now to cancel my visa and then get ourselves out!

All liabilities under my name had been cleared ...or so I thought! Another visit to immigration to perform the final step of cancelling my visa now led me to be told that my visa could not be cancelled as long as Amalia was on a tourist visa. She would have to leave the country first in order to complete her tourist visa, after which time, my visa would be cancelled.

So close yet so far. I had to tell Rwanda that I was still unable to get out of Qatar. I couldn't explain why. How could they possibly understand what I would have to say? And so, they waited. Eventually after many more trips to immigration, a very helpful English-speaking captain assisted me in my plight. He saw that Amalia was not yet one year old. She could not depart Qatar without me. His heavy hand stamped cancelled on Amalia's tourist visa and then seconds later the same hand cancelled my visa. Fourteen months after I had been fired from my job, I was free to leave Qatar.

Thinking of you

Susan

MULTIPLE FATHERS

August 2008-May 2009, Doha, Qatar, Stockholm, Sweden, Frankfurt, Germany, Male, Maldives, Doha, Qatar.

"An eye for an eye will only make the whole world blind."
Gandhi

Dear mum.

I went to have an amniocentesis in a government hospital in Qatar. The proceedings that led up to the need for an amniocentesis are relatively obvious, however as with everything your only daughter undertakes, there is naturally a story behind the lead up.

I had fallen for someone who I perceived to be quite exotic. He worked as a cabin crew for the major airline in Qatar. He was typically tall, dark, and handsome. When he travelled out of Qatar we would talk and when he was in Qatar we would go out for dinner and watch movies.

Our relationship developed and whenever he was in Doha, we would be together. He would give me his flight schedule in order for me to know when he would be on the ground, and I could plan myself around that. Then he started coordinating his long-haul layovers in a way that I could join him on the flight, enjoy the luxury of a five-star hotel in a foreign destination and see places I had always dreamed of.

Our first destination was Stockholm, Sweden. Three amazing days in an amazing city. We travelled on the same flight. He brought me food and chocolates from the first-class cabin and making sure I had the most comfortable seats in economy. The weather was freezing and my journey by train from the airport to the hotel where I was to meet him, I almost froze to death in my shirt and trousers from Qatar. I remember stopping to buy takeout coffee on the street and within seconds the steaming heat had turned to ice cold latte. Our hotel was the Sheraton, right in the heart of downtown Stockholm. Amazing views and right next to the old quarter, with its quaint cobblestone streets and dainty tea shops with open fires burning inside.

Following the trip to Sweden, our next destination out of Doha was Frankfurt. The weather was beautiful, and the sunshine brought everyone outside to eating venues in old squares surrounded by buildings older than I could ever have imagined. Three days flew by in Germany and before we knew it, we were back in Doha. That was however not the end of our exotic holidaying adventures. Our next destination was the island paradise of the Maldives. Another three-day layover and we were back to the reality of work and life in Doha.

This story seems like the long way around to get to the point of the amnio, however what it actually is, is the sequence of events that led up to the need for the amnio. I found out I was pregnant at 12 weeks. Of course, subconsciously I already knew, but the reality of being in an Arab country, pregnant, and not married was an issue I was not particularly willing to face. Eventually after taking the test and then confirming the result with the doctor, at age 39, I was expecting my first child!

Doctors in Qatar are very strict about genetic screening tests for pregnant women, especially ones my age. Many thoughts were swimming around in my head. The first thing the doctor in our private clinic said was "I hope you have a marriage certificate!" As my heart sank, I obviously replied with a confident "well of course!" The appointment was booked for the amniocentesis to take place in a government hospital in Doha. I had no idea what to expect. I had done no reading up on the procedure and only knew that there would be a tough decision to make if there was a positive result for a genetic abnormality.

There were still a couple of obstacles that would need to be overcome before I even got to the appointment. The lesser one was the fact that on the day of the appointment we had school inspectors coming into work and had been vehemently threatened by our boss that we were not to be absent. Although I was nervous about that, it was the least of my worries. The more pressing issue was the fact that in order to open a file in the government hospital I would need to present a marriage certificate for them to open a file and provide treatment.

The father of the baby had already disappeared by this point, and even if he was around, a marriage certificate was not going to be the answer. I had spent hours crying with a dear friend over the entire situation and we came up with the solution of marrying a dear mutual friend who would be happy to oblige. That however was not to be. Foreigners getting married in Qatar is difficult. There is no Australian embassy and the laws on marriage are Islamic. We googled going to another country, but all was just too difficult, as time was ticking and the appointment date approaching rapidly.

There was one final option. A last-ditch effort. It was a long shot, but at this point I was almost fourteen weeks pregnant and was happy to exhaust every available possibility.

Mr. Kenya and I had been divorced about two years prior to this sequence of events. We had been married in Kenya, but our divorce was processed in Australia. In those proceedings, the government had not asked for the marriage certificate to be returned to the office. Therefore, it was still in my possession. My last-ditch effort was to ask Mr. Kenya if I could use it for this purpose.

We drove to the corniche in Al Khor and sat in the car watching the ocean and Arab fishing boats hauling their days work. I took a deep breath and then told him the story of my being pregnant and needing to go for this procedure, which I needed a marriage certificate for. In Qatar if you are pregnant outside of marriage you are imprisoned. When you give birth, the baby was taken to an orphanage and you, the mother, are deported from the country. So, what I was asking this ex-husband of mine was somewhat important!

After hearing the facts, Mr. Kenya took a deep breath and said "Susan, you know I would do anything for you!" Of course, I burst into tears. Went home, dug out that marriage certificate, which was now a piece of paper that was keeping me from either side of a set of prison bars and prepared to attend the appointment the following morning.

Very early on the day of the appointment, I woke and drove myself the 60 kilometers to the hospital. I truly believed that I would be in and out in no time and back at work for the inspection. Little did I know! I arrived and completed all documentation pertaining to the file. The marriage certificate was placed meticulously inside the file, with the value of a piece of gold. I was escorted upstairs where I was left to sit outside the clinic with lots of other women.

Dressed in a black and white shirt with black T-shirt, I was sitting at the end of a row of chairs reading my novel which just happened to be about the history of Islamic women. I was the only non-Islamic woman in the room. As I turned my head and looked along the row of seats where I sat, every woman was covered from head to toe in black. No fingertips could be seen, and eyes were fully covered by the deep black cloth of their abaya. In my head I thought, "Which girl from Adelaide has ever had this experience?"

And so, the amniocentesis was conducted. I lay on the table looking at the ceiling and repeating Tashania and Aaliyah's names, knowing that a large part of what I was doing was for them. After a painful six week wait for the results, I was finally called and told that the results were clear and that the baby was healthy.

Love Susan

CHANCE ENCOUNTER

April 2010 Qatar Airways flight from Nairobi, Kenya to Doha, Qatar.

"Anyone can have a child and call themselves a parent. A real parent is someone who puts that child above their own selfish needs and wants." Unknown

Dear Mum

I met Marley's birth father. As you already know, after Mr. Kenya agreed to help me out with the marriage certificate, he offered so much more. He agreed to be Marley's father and to raise him as he raises Tashania and Aaliyah. They are all his children. The transfer of blood does not make a person a mother or father. Neither does the donation of sperm. A father is the person who is going to love the child unconditionally, who is going to provide for the child and guide them to be the best people they can be. Three of my children are so fortunate to have a father who guides them, provides for them, and loves them unconditionally. The bonds that tie them together are so strong that the blood they do not share between any of them is insignificant.

Mr. Kenya moved back into the house and supported me throughout the pregnancy. He massaged my feet and went out to buy peppermint ice cream whenever it was required. When Marley was born, Mr. Kenya was there. Although he was in the emergency room himself because he was so overcome with shock that he believed himself to be in a worse position than I was, and as I was about to be taken to theatre for the c-section, he announces that he is so sick that he needs to go to the emergency room to be treated. Nevertheless, he was there. Marley got his surname, the same as the girls, and life began.

Mr. Kenya was a hands-on father. He would bathe the baby, feed him, and take him for walks early on a Saturday morning so I could sleep in. When Marley was six months old, we decided to take a family holiday back to Kenya. We had taken many such trips in our life and this one was no different. Visiting family and friends. Eating in our favorite restaurants and enjoying every minute in the country we all love so much.

Our time had come to an end and before we knew it, we were on our flight returning to Doha. I had an aisle seat, with the girls next to me and Marley on my lap. After take-off, he was particularly restless and being so squashed, I decided to wrap him in his sleepy wrap and walk up and down the aisle, praying that before too long he would be asleep.

I started walking down the aisle towards the back of the plane. When I got to the row of seats next to the toilets, I noticed a good friend of mine sitting in the aisle seat. Right next to him was Marley's biological father! He met his son for the first time flying at thirty-five thousand feet on a flight from Nairobi to Doha. The look on his face was nothing short of a combination

44

of shock and terror. Shock at the cuteness of this child and terror at the thought of what the child's mother could do to him in this plane. He had walked out on me the day he found out I was expecting a baby. I had never seen him since. I said hi, introduced him to his son, and chatted briefly before turbulence came and we needed to return to our seat. Back with my family. I knew that was where I was meant to be.

Trusting you are all well.

Love Susan

MASSAGE MADNESS

End of April 2010

"Integrity: A name is the blueprint of the thing we call character. You ask, What's in a name? Just about everything you do." Morris Mandel

Dear Mum,

As someone who has travelled the world, I have taken a particular liking to getting a massage in different countries. Living in Malaysia, there was not a huge amount to do on weekends, so it was a regular pastime of expat ladies to go and get a very cheap massage before spending the rest of the day lying by the Hyatt Hotel pool. Massage can be quite addictive. As the number of children in my family grew and the cost of massage increased in the different countries, I lived in the frequency of getting a regular massage reduced.

When Marley was about six months old, I really felt like I needed a massage. It was still tricky to find the time to get out of the house so a friend of mine connected with someone on the internet to arrange a home visit. Bearing in mind that we are living in the conservative country of Qatar, a home visit massage by a person called Michelle did not seem to pose much of a problem. Most massage therapists in Qatar came from the Philippines and they were usually quite good at the art of massage.

So, there is a knock at the door and as I open it, I see a rather large, hairy man of Arabic ethnicity. I ask if he is Michelle, and he replies in a deep husky voice that he is! I start to shake but feel that he has come all this way and perhaps I should not judge a book by its cover. I welcome him in and as he is proceeding up the stairs to the bedroom where the massage will take place, I turn around and mouth to Marley's dad that he is not to leave the place where he is sitting until I have finished!

Michelle and I go upstairs and enter the spare bedroom. I undress and lie down on the bed with a towel wrapped around me ready for the massage to begin. Michelle then sits down on the bed and with an enormous thud, the bed breaks! At this point Marley's father who is sitting downstairs comes up and asks if everything is alright. A somewhat muffled reply from me indicates that for now it was bearable. Having broken the bed with his body weight, Michelle then asks me if he could smoke! As I almost choke on nothing in my mouth and in my head thinking, "People usually do that after not before...don't they" I replied that it would not be OK, and he should wait until he has finished.

Having established the rules of massage Michelle then begins. He moves the towel away from my legs and puts a healthy amount of massage oil onto his palms. As his hands move up my legs from the ankles to the upper thigh, Michelle lets out this uncomfortably loud grunting noise. I am shocked and grab hold of the bed sheets tightly. He continues the massage, with the same movements on my legs and the grunts get louder and more frequent. My entire body is now clenched tightly, and my fingers are about to bleed from the nails digging into clenched fists. I didn't know what to do! I knew I wanted this to end but did not want to appear rude. I was praying that Mr. Kenya would walk into the room to see if everything was going well, but he was too absorbed in his television programme. After one particularly loud grunt I jumped up from the bed insisting that I could hear the baby crying. Grabbing onto the towel I raced down the stairs and told Mr. Kenya to get that man out of the house. Mr. Kenya could see that I was visibly upset and didn't ask any questions. He simply went upstairs and explained that the baby needed me, and that Michelle should leave.

The next morning my friend who had arranged this massage sent me a message asking how the massage had gone. Still in shock I asked how he had found this person. He then revealed that he had located him on the internet. When I asked if he had ever spoken to Michelle over the phone before setting up this appointment, he said no. Then I said Michelle was a guy! Explained the massage to him and left it at that! No more home massages for me!

Lots of Love

Susan

ARABIAN BEAUTY

2005-2015, Doha, Qatar, Al Khor, Qatar

"Beauty is like a book...it cannot be judged by its cover."
Unknown

Dear Mum

Over the course of my life, I have come to learn we live in a society governed by fear. Fear of the unknown, fear of something or someone we don't fully understand. The media propagates this fear through their stories and the way in which they tell them. I remember once when I was visiting Australia from Qatar and Simon, his family, and I went to Queensland on holiday. Simon and I had popped out to the local grocery store for supplies. As we were standing in the line at the checkout, the lady in front of us was covered from head to toe in a black abaya. Simon lent over to me and told me that he feared these people. I didn't see this perceived fear as a reflection of Simon. This is what he and many others have been encultured to believe about those who are different.

So, I thought I would write and tell you a little bit about Arab women, Muslim women. Women who when they go out in public are completely covered from head to toe in an abaya. At the time that I lived in Qatar there were one million people. Two hundred thousand were Qatari and eight hundred thousand were expatriate workers who were employed to work in all areas across the country.

From my experience, there was very little interpersonal interaction between Qatari and ex-patriots. The society was still quite a closed one and it was rare for a Westerner to get to see the inside workings of family life and culture.

I got a job teaching English privately to university students. These students were all women. They had attended secondary school that was entirely in Arabic and were now at university that was full English medium. These were a group of extremely intelligent women who had high aspirations for themselves. They were studying to be interior designers, diplomats, and lawyers. Their only academic downfall was the fact that their intelligence was being evaluated through the medium of English. The ladies could all speak English, however writing an academic essay to the conventions of a Western university standard was another story. Often, I would have a look through the text of readings and find that my student had needed to translate the entire document into Arabic in order to understand it. I was amazed at the brilliance of these women.

One of my students was studying international relations. She had to write an essay on the oppression of Arab women. The texts she had to read were all very American feminist-based texts. As my student translated and read through a large section of such texts, she still had no comprehension of what they were about. This was not due to a language difficulty, this was purely the result of the fact that my student, an Arab woman could not relate in any way to what was being written in these texts by American women.

So, our lesson began with me telling my student about the perceptions that many Western women have of Arab women or more specifically women who wear an abaya. I explained that Western women were led to believe that Arab women had no rights of their own, that they were purely dominated by the actions of men, and that they wore the abaya as a symbol of patriarchal oppression. As I continued with my definition, my student just started laughing. Her life experience could not have been further from the truth.

Yes, she lived in a very conservative house and yes, her parents would choose a husband for her, however as the lesson continued, she began to tell me exactly what her rights were. She had decided that she would not get married until she had finished university. Her mother who was younger than me had not attended school. In fact, her mother had grown up in a Bedouin lifestyle. She lived in a tent in the desert. Raised sheep and had no access to formal education.

Qatar as we know it today is very new. It was only thirty-five years ago that gas was discovered in this tiny country. Before this Qataris were predominantly pearl fishermen. They lived a Bedouin lifestyle with no access to the riches that Qataris have today. With the discovery of gas, Qataris literally overnight became the richest nation per capita in the world. The government of Qatar shares the wealth with the people many of whom now lead the most opulent lifestyles imaginable. Huge fancy houses and cars, financial assistance for weddings, mortgages, and travel. There was a time when the government would collect around two hundred cars a month that had simply been left by their owners on the side of the road after being involved in an accident. For some Qataris, it was easier to go and buy a new car than worry about the hassle of getting this one repaired. These cars would then be taken to second-hand car markets where they would be sold for spare parts. My son, who left Qatar at the age of four, would frequently say as we were driving along "Look, Mummy, a Lamborghini! Or why don't we see how many Porsches we can count on our way to town!"

So, my student was very determined to get a university education. Her parents were equally as determined for this to happen and did everything within their power to offer her their support. They knew that she was of marriageable age, however, they also respected her wish to finish university before she settled into marriage. So, prospective suitors would come to the house. Suitors who had been sent by other family members or friends. People who knew this girl was of marriageable age. Of course, being an Arabic culture, the suitor would not be permitted to see the girl. In fact, at this early stage of the arrangements, she would probably not even enter the room where he was seated. However, if she did, she would be fully covered in her abaya, and he would be entitled to see nothing but her height.

So, suitors would come with their parents and be greeted in the traditional Qatari style of food, Arabic coffee, and sweets. They would be entertained, treated with the utmost respect, and leave. My student would then refuse the proposal. For she and her parents knew she was not going to get married until she had finished university. These moves were really a matter of tradition. She however was the one with complete control over when she was going to get married. Not the man and not her parents.

Finally, after three years of working with this student, she graduated from university with a degree in International Relations.

52

Together we had written essays on Machiavelli, theories of international diplomacy and the oppression of Arabic women! More importantly we had built a bond with each other. She had let me into her world, and I had exposed her to mine. We had sat for hours drinking Arabic coffee, strong and flavoured with cardamom from the tiny cups. Its bitterness was sweetened by the most expensive chocolates that would always be a centerpiece on the table where we sat for our lessons. She taught me to wobble my cup when I no longer wanted more coffee and I taught her about the customs of a world far removed from that of her own. For me I felt like an anthropologist on National Geographic who studies African cultures from the inside. And this student was only one of many who took me inside her world.

Her sister, who was also a student of mine, once invited my children and I went out to a mall with them. She said she just wanted to spend time with us.

It was during the Holy month of Ramadan where Muslims fast from eating or drinking between sunlight and sunset. In Qatar Ramadan fell during the hottest part of the year. When the days were long and light for many hours. Ramadan in Qatar was very different to the Ramadan we had previously experienced in Malaysia. In Malaysia, life continued as normal. Non-Muslims still ate and drank, restaurants remained open during the day, and the Muslim people demonstrated their dedication to their faith as part of their daily lives. In Qatar, Ramadan turned day into night and night into day. During daylight hours, all the restaurants were closed. Non-Muslims were not permitted to eat or drink in public. School and office hours would be reduced so the Muslim people could go home and sleep. At school, we would have fasting and non-fasting lunchrooms where our students who were eating would be barricaded inside with windows blackened out so they could have their lunch.

During Ramadan Muslims break their fast when a call to prayer announces that the moon has been sighted. So, my student broke her fast with her family and then we headed to the mall at around 9pm. It was amazing the way people stared at us as we were eating and shopping. My student was fully adorned in her abaya, and I was wearing my regular clothes. This was simply not a common sight to be seen in Qatar. A Western lady and an Arab woman dressed in her abaya socializing together. It was another truly unique moment for me.

Now getting back to my first student who had now finished university and was in a position to get married. I walked into my office at work and saw a white box on my desk. It was about 50cms high and equally wide. It was white, with a red bow and some of those expensive chocolates attached to the top. I carefully untied the bow and opened the lid. Inside was a wooden Arabic style door. Opening the two wooden flaps on the front of the door revealed exquisite gold, Arabic style calligraphy. I took the wedding invitation to an Arabic speaker who told me that this was an invite to the wedding of my student. My colleague also read the name of the groom. He was also a student who I had worked with briefly on a work presentation of his. More importantly than that, he was her first cousin! The bride and groom had grown up together. His father and her mother were brother and sister from the same mother and father (such a point is always important in my world, because so often people claim to be brothers and sisters for many cultural reasons when, in fact, they may be cousins or have no blood relation and simply have been raised in the same house). They lived next door to each other and obviously knew each other inside out. His parents had gone through the ritual of offering their son to my student and at this time in her life, she had accepted.

To marry a first cousin in Qatar is not seen as something to be frowned upon as it is in the West. In situations such as this families know exactly what they are getting themselves in for. The bride's family knows the economic, social, religious, and moral status of the groom and his family and everyone is clear from the onset. The Qatari government has put a system of genetic screening in place for all couples who are to marry. This has been done to lessen the outcome of birth defects in children who are born to couples who are so closely related.

A Qatari wedding is very different to a Western wedding. The first part of the ceremony is when the groom's family brings copious amounts of gold to the bride's family. I was told that the starting price of this offering is around one hundred thousand Australian dollars. This gold acts as symbols of security for the bride should anything go wrong.

Love Susan

CRASH!

July 2013,

Doha, Qatar, Bangkok, Thailand, Han Oi, Vietnam, Kuantan, Malaysia, Kuala Lumpur, Malaysia, Chiang Mai, Thailand

"What we imagine is order is merely the prevailing form of chaos.: Kerry Thornley.

Dear Mum.

In July of 2013, yet another Asian adventure was to begin. It was Mr. Rwanda's first trip out of Africa and the Middle East and our first big trip together. Our itinerary had us landing in Bangkok. We would then fly to Vietnam, Malaysia, and back to Thailand, where we would take the overnight train from Bangkok to Chiang Mai. This was a part of the trip I was particularly enthusiastic about. I had never explored this area of Thailand and was fascinated by the prospect of meeting the Hill Tribe people, elephant trekking through the jungles and rafting on bamboo rafts.

The overnight train ride was an exciting part of the trip that we had been looking forward to since we had made the booking. Trains are such a great way to travel long distances with young children because they are self-contained, and the children can move freely. The added bonus of our seats converting to bunk beds at night made the whole experience feel like an exotic adventure. I have always had a fondness for trains ever since I had taken the overnight train from Nairobi to Mombasa in my early days in Kenya. At the time of booking, I had wanted to reserve the first-class section, however due to the fact that it was fully booked, I settled for second-class.

The Bangkok train station was a typically busy place to be, with both regular and long-distance travelers scrambling through crowds to find the correct train. After locating our twenty-one-cabin long train we stood in front of our cabin to take an obligatory travel photography. Little did we know at this time that this would be one of the last photographs taken of this train carriage.

As we settled into our booth the children quickly made friends with the German children sitting next to us who were similar in age to mine. Not long after we departed from Bangkok, the waiter came around to serve dinner. There was an option to have dinner in the dining carriage; however we decided to convert our booth into our dining room by assembling the table, between the two booth seats. At this stage of our adventure, we were also not aware that this very table would play a part in potentially saving our lives.

After our delicious Thai meal in our fabulous surroundings, the train staff came around to clear the tables and set about transforming the seats into our overnight bunk beds. The children were so excited at this point. Two seats folded downwards, and a board and mattress were placed on top. Luggage was carefully tucked into overhead compartments and the children got into their sleeping gear and climbed into their respective bunks. Aaliyah on the top and Marley on the bottom. Perhaps the rocking motion of the train helped them to sleep as they were quickly off, giving us time to sit and enjoy a drink before retiring to our bunks ourselves.

At 3am we were woken by a thunderous crashing sound and found ourselves thrown out of our bunk beds. Our carriage, along with about twenty others had disengaged from the first-class cabins while it was moving up hill and had subsequently plummeted down the hill and fallen completely off the tracks. The cabin now sideways meant that for us to stand the floor was now what had been our window side of the train. I frantically searched for Marley and Aaliyah. I found Aaliyah first. She always slept curled up like a tiny ball and stood up covered in blankets obviously very confused. I couldn't see through the darkness and panicked that Marley was not OK, He had been sleeping alone on the lower bunk. I screamed for him, and his head popped up from underneath a pile of blankets and bags that were now strewn all over the floor. Both children were fine, despite being thrown from their beds. Mr. Rwanda and I both looked at each other in the confusion and automatically thought of water. Water and rivers are everywhere in Thailand and if this train was about to slide into water, we would all be dead.

When I first travelled to Kenya in 1990. I had been part of a teenage exchange program where teenagers were billeted with families in Nairobi and Mombasa for nine weeks. I had always wanted to go to Africa and one freezing cold evening in Adelaide, when I was playing netball one of my teammates mentioned that she was going to China as a supervisor on a teenage exchange program. The company she was going with also had exchanges in Kenya and Russia. In exchange for your services of supervising and coordinating activities for the teenagers, the supervisors got nine weeks free accommodation. While we had to pay for our own plane tickets, this seemed like the perfect way for me to fulfill my childhood dream of travelling to Africa. So, I got the contacts of the Adelaide based company, attended the training sessions, was accepted and off I went. Thirty teenagers and five staff members.

In those nine weeks, I probably travelled between Nairobi and Mombasa three times for various reasons. The third time was just before the group was travelling back to Australia. I had decided to extend my trip and stay on for an extra month after the rest of the group had departed. I decided to change my return train journey from Thursday to the Wednesday before as it would give me more time to arrange things in Nairobi. My train journey was as smooth and enjoyable as they had always been. The train pulled into the Nairobi Railway Station at 6am and I went about my daily duties.

The following day, just a couple of days before the entire group's departure for Australia, the students who were on our program all boarded the train for their return to Nairobi. Sadly, that train never made it to Nairobi. Just outside of the inland town of Voi, a bridge that was undergoing repairs collapsed as the train crossed over it, plummeting into the water. Luckily, none of our students were killed, but recounts of their experiences told us how their carriages had been submerged in water and many of them had had to escape through the openings of windows as the water rose towards the surface. With no belongings, our students had swum through the crocodile infested water to the shore to await rescue. Search parties were sent from Nairobi in helicopters to get our students back safely.

Unfortunately for many others on the train their life's journey ended in that river.

So now here we were nearly twenty years later. It was 3am and we were trapped inside the cabin of an overturned train in the jungles of Northern Thailand. Mr. Rwanda immediately went into rescue mode. He is very good at responding to emergency situations. He grabbed the table that we had used to eat our Thai dinner on and as the cabin steward rubbed his sleepy eyes and walked towards us, went to smash it through the window that had now become our roof. The cabin steward tried to stop him, saying that it would be better for us to wait inside the cabin. Mr. Rwanda did not agree with these sentiments and proceeded to smash the thick glass of the window with the blunt end of the ironing board shaped table. The children and I covered our heads with our hands as shattered glass fell all around us.

With an opening in the roof of the train, Mr. Rwanda lifted Marley and rested him outside the top of the train. I was next to be hoisted out. The terror in me was immense. I still thought the train could continue to tip and slide into the water. I was refusing to get out. Mr. Rwanda calmly put his hands together for me to slip my feet into. I did as he said and within minutes I too was on the roof of the train with Marley. Aaliyah who is as light as a feather was lifted next. As shock set into her, her teeth chattered, and her body shook violently. With the three of us now on the roof of the train, Mr. Rwanda joined us to ascertain how we would now get off the train. He jumped down onto the tracks to survey the area.

There was only one train line, so no other train could get through. The air was hot and humid, and mosquitoes buzzed frantically. Mr. Rwanda navigated the three of us off the train, using the wheels as steps to lower ourselves onto the track.

After lowering us down, he went to get the others from our cabin out. Some other men and their families were now on the track and were trying to check the surrounding area for danger. At one point a person who had come out of another cabin shouted that a train was coming, sending everyone fleeing into the jungle. This panic quickly subsided, and everyone sat themselves down on the train track, waiting for morning and hopefully a rescue team to come and collect us. Mr. Rwanda went back into the train to collect people's belongings and managed to salvage some bed sheets and blankets that the children could use to sleep on and to protect themselves from mosquitoes. I made a bed for Marley, nuzzled between the train tracks, with some blood-stained sheets and blankets and thankfully for all, he slept until the sun came up. Aaliyah was reunited with her German friends on the train tracks and their mum kept the children busy with songs and games. Mr. Rwanda helped treat some of the wounded passengers.

By daybreak, a rescue train had arrived about a kilometer away. Injured people were taken away first, followed by the rest of the passengers. About six hours later we were in a tiny Thai village where the train company had arranged buses to transport us to Chiang Mai. The local people were incredibly kind. They fed us, gave us drinks and let us use their bathrooms. Exhausted but happy to be alive, we boarded the coach for the five-hour journey into Chiang Mai. Upon arrival there, we were given no explanation as to what had happened. In fact, passengers simply gathered their belongings, got into nearby taxis, headed off to their next destinations. We only found out any details about the train crash the next day when it was headline news in the local newspaper.

Our time in Chiang Mai was filled with mixed emotions. While we still enjoyed visiting the hill tribe people, elephant riding, and river rafting, all we really wanted to do was get back to some more familiar territory. After a few days, we took our flight back to Kuala Lumpur. The first thing I did was go to a chemist. Early the next morning I opened the package I had bought at the chemist...

Love Susan

GIFTS AND NIGHTMARES

July 2013-February 2019

Amalia means "A Gift from God"

Dear Mum

As we sat between the railway tracks in the jungles of Northern Thailand, I already knew. Bodies and chaos were all around us. Parents comforting their children. Marley curled up in blood-soaked bed sheets between the tracks was luckily fast asleep and Aaliyah was happily playing in the darkness with some of the other children. However, although I already knew, now was not the time or place to be confirming or denying it.

Arriving back in Kuala Lumpur a few days later was a different story. KL was like home. I knew how to navigate my way around KL and could confidently access anything I needed. We checked into our hotel. A luxurious suite on the twenty fifth floor of an inner-city hotel. Dinner of Malaysian satay and roti channai was familiar and delicious. As Mr. Rwanda took

Aaliyah and Marley into an enormous candy store, I popped into the pharmacy for a quick over-the-counter purchase, before joining them and heading back to the hotel.

I had been clear in my mind that I had not wanted him to know what I was doing. I woke up early the next morning, opened my bag, and went into the bathroom, locking the door behind me. I had only ever done one of these tests once before and as I opened the package and unfolded the instructions, I realized that the writing was too small for me to read, and my glasses had gone missing in the train crash.

In a bit of a panic now, I unlocked the bathroom door and found he was awake. In whispered tones so as not to wake up the children, I handed him the box and asked him to read the instructions and tell me what I needed to do. I followed the instructions and the two of us sat on the edge of the bed watching the stick change colour.

This was still a new relationship, and I was under no illusions about the fact that this was not a match made in heaven. He had spent most nights of this trip exploring the night life of the various cities we had visited and all they had to offer. On the first night of arrival in Bangkok, he had left us in the hotel room and disappeared. He had no local currency, no local phone number and was not even clear of our hotel address, and yet, as he continued to do on many nights throughout the trip, he disappeared for hours.

On that night I had awoken with severe stomach cramps. Thinking it was from having been sitting on a plane for many hours, I vomited a few times, awakening each time to find him not there in the room.

After picking myself up from the bathroom floor for the fifth time, I called him on his international phone line and told him that it was probably in everyone's best interest for him to get back to the hotel. Drunk and unremorseful, he staggered back to the hotel room a few hours later and collapsed into bed. In hindsight I should have realized at the time that this was a pattern he was bringing into the relationship from his previous ones and that this was to be a pattern I would endure during the entire six years we were together. Instead, I pulled on my cape of denial and convinced myself that I would be worthy enough for him to change those behaviors. But as I have come to realize as time with him went on, the conscious and unconscious minds are often not that aligned.

As the pregnancy test revealed a positive result, my heart raced, and my stomach caved in. I collapsed to the ground, head in hands, sobbing. He on the other hand danced around the room in a state of sheer pleasure. While possibly not the pleasure other fathers would experience upon the news of a new baby, this one was more the pleasure associated with the conquering of new territory. Conquering the height of Mount Kilimanjaro. I was forty-three years old when I found out I was pregnant with Amalia. At least I was healthy, both physically and financially, or so I thought.

We went back to Qatar and moved forward through a healthy pregnancy. It was not until I returned to Australia five years later that I really became familiar with the term narcissist. This occurred in the midst of my brokenness, literally on my knees when a post came up on my Facebook feed that resonated. It was called "Five signs to tell if your partner is a narcissist." As I completed the quiz and scored a perfect ten, potentially confirming two things. One that my partner was a narcissist and two that he was never really my partner because narcissists are incapable of being in a partnership.

So, while I was physically healthy during the pregnancy, the way it messed with his image of himself caused extreme suffering to everyone in my house. You see I was of the cultural understanding that as a pregnant woman it was kind of a rite of passage to be taken extra care of. Well, as was to be the case with all my preconceived perceptions of how relationships operate, I was very wrong.

You see, for a narcissist, they have to be the center of attention at all costs. Their fractured relationship with themselves means they are constantly seeking external validation of their worth. So, as I thought I would be getting a bit of extra special care and attention, so did he...from anyone who was willing to offer it. His infidelity had been rife since we met, however I was not to fully understand the extent of it until much later.

Some friends had given us a weekend away at a beautiful hotel in Doha. I was about six months pregnant at the time. While I had imagined us having a nice meal together, taking a walk along the Corniche and perhaps watching a movie, he had other plans. Upon arrival at the hotel, he started taking photographs of himself and sending them to his friends. As he then engaged them in texting conversations, he began to invite them over to the hotel to come into our room and drink with him. As my anger rose, I decided to express to him what I thought this weekend was meant to be about. After all it was the last time, we would be together as a couple before the baby was born...Knockout...Standing my ground was not appreciated! Expecting us to be together without his friends or without his alcohol was not appreciated. As I tried to defend myself and my position tensions continued to rise, and he dealt with this the only way he knew how. I was knocked to the floor and as I clutched my swollen belly, he stepped over me, opened the door and left to go and prowl the streets of Doha with his friends.

He had always wanted a daughter. His first wife had given him three sons with huge age gaps in between. We decided that instead of going through the government-based hospital system that I had done with Marley, we would go private. I had anticipated having another amniocentesis as I had done with Marley and was prepared for that. As it happened, the Sudanese doctor who had performed my amniocentesis had left the government system and gone private. Through him we went for a series of 4D scans and based on the results of these, decided that this was evidence enough for us not to do the amniocentesis. The only time I have ever seen this man shed tears was when our doctor turned his head away from the television monitor and told him it was a girl. That day, he held my hand as we walked out of the doctor's office and got into the car.

At five months pregnant I travelled to Kenya for business. I was building up a successful recruitment agency where I was bringing Kenyan ladies to Qatar to work for ex patriot families as domestic helpers. It was only a four-and-a-half-hour flight between Doha and Nairobi, and I travelled this route frequently.

I had pre-arranged to meet and interview potential candidates the following Saturday morning. Each lady had entered my office, registered their details, listened to my presentation, and met with me individually. All except one lady who snuck out silently after my presentation to wait outside in her car. It wasn't until later that day that I had found out who she was. She had refused to register her full details, instead opting to ask my receptionist only one question...Was I pregnant!

The meetings went well, and many ladies expressed their interest in getting jobs in Qatar. They were all single mothers themselves and many were professionals. In Kenya they were not able to find work in their selected fields and even if there was a job there it paid less than going to Qatar as a housemaid would pay them.

After the meeting I fare welled my staff, got into my car, and headed way across town to a mall right next door to the friend's house I was staying at. Desperate for some lunch and a cold passion juice, I decided to quickly race through the super-market to pick up some things I needed, and then trolley fully laden, head to my favorite coffee shop to sit down, digest the day, and enjoy a lovely meal.

The courtyard seating area was empty, and I took a seat near the window to the building, so I had somewhere to strategically position my trolley. As I looked at the menu a middle-aged man wearing a shabby mitumba suit came and sat down at my table, asking if he could join me. While it is common for Kenyans to squeeze themselves into seating areas where people are already sitting, this was really quite unusual because the restaurant was pretty much empty.

I knew Kenya better than many Kenyans. I had once sat in a coffee shop on Kimathi Street having been approached by a man asking me if he could buy me a cup of coffee. This was in my early years there and being friendly I obliged. I had just come out of the nearby Barclays Bank where I had changed some foreign currency into Kenyan Shillings. The man started telling me that he was a refugee from South Africa. On his way to Djibouti and needed money for the fare. He said I would be personally thanked by Desmond Tutu for saving someone from near death. It was unusual because for someone who said he was not from Kenya, he was certainly very familiar with all the waiters in this restaurant, who greeted him with fist bumps and handshakes, smiles, and grinning widely with the smell of freshly converted cash.

I however was a bit sharper than they were giving me credit for. I asked to be excused to use the bathroom and once inside I took the wad of tightly rolled cash out of my pocket, removed my shoes and carefully lay notes into the sole of both my shoes. I came out of the bathroom with just enough cash to cover my bill, dropped it on the table and excused myself for another engagement.

Then there was the time when my friends had been sitting at an outdoor café in Nairobi and a man came and joined them. Minutes later, other men pretending to be police showed up at the table while the first man disappeared quickly. The second two said the first man was a political troublemaker and that because they were friends with him, they would be arrested. As these girls protested the insanity of this, the 'policemen' said that if the girls paid them a huge amount of cash, they would be free to go. Not having that cash on them, the 'policemen' escorted the girls to the bank, waited outside and within minutes the girls came out, handed over a huge amount of cash and were released.

The waiter came to collect the order from this stranger and me. The stranger looked up from the menu and said to the waiter that he would have a glass of warm tap water. Alarm bells are now firing around me like sirens. I ordered my lunch, left my trolley where it was positioned and excused myself to use the bathroom. As I entered the interior of the restaurant, I explained to the waiters that I did not know this man and had no idea why he was sitting at my table. They had obviously assumed we were together. I asked them to give me a table in the restaurant and to bring my trolley inside. The stranger, thrown off balance by my departure from the table eventually left the restaurant. One of the waiters escorted me to my car and helped me put my shopping inside. Ignition on, doors locked, I got home safely.

In a conversation that evening with my receptionist, where I retold the events of the stranger in the coffee shop, she told me about the strange lady who came to the interviews in the morning and refused to give any of her details, only asking if I was pregnant. Through a couple of other conversations and some very strange text messages that came through to my phone that evening, we managed to figure out the unusual events of the day. The woman who had come for the interviews was his mistress of roughly sixteen years. While his Kenyan wife had remained little competition for this woman, I on the other hand was a different story. This woman knew she would lose him and that all the money in the world would not put her in a position to compete with a mzungu. She had pretended to be a prospective housemaid looking for a job really just to see me and put together her plan of attack. She had left the office and waited in her car for me to leave and then she had followed me to the coffee shop. She had planted the man to come and sit at the table with me in anticipation that I would not be as aware as I was and would have engaged him in a conversation, perhaps even offering to buy him lunch. He would then have put some form of drug into my drink and who knows what the outcome would have been.

It was not until I returned to Australia many years after this incident that I came to fully understand the ways in which narcissists use triangulation to feed into their own sense of importance. Of course, it was he who had told this woman I would be in Nairobi. He had given her the address of my office and the timing that I would be there. For him, this level of insanity was something that gave him so much greatly required narcissistic supply that any sense of consequence went unheeded.

The day before Amalia was born (although I had not realized, she would be born the day after), I needed to get my car registered. In Qatar in those days, you had to firstly get it road tested, then the insurance and registration were done at two separate offices in town. I drove about 17kms out of Al Khor to a place in the absolute middle of the desert. Nothing but sand and gravel surrounded the outdoor venue, where people lined up in their cars waiting for a policeman who would conduct the inspection. When my turn came, I stood out in the desert, sand blowing everywhere, my belly heavy and my feet swollen. The policemen were kind and quickly inspected the car and sent me back into town to start the paperwork for the registration.

I joined the line at the Al Khor motor registration department and was quickly moved to the front of the line due to my condition. I handed over my passport to a lady smiling behind the creases of her face covering. I had lived in Qatar for such a long time that I knew how to read the facial expressions of the ladies who were covered from head to toe in black fabric. It was all in their eyes. She typed away at the screen and then pulled off a receipt and said that I had a fine that would need to be paid before I could register the car. The fine was 14,000 Qatari Riyals. The equivalent of around $5000. Absolutely stunned I asked the lady if she could please explain what these fines were for. This was a huge amount of money and having been with this man for almost a year, I had been financially drained of every last penny. I was told there were two red lights at 5000 Qatari Riyals each and multiple speeding fines. At that moment, my knees gave way and I fell to the floor. This really was too much. I had no money to pay this bill and now would be without a car when I was due to give birth any day. Two police ladies escorted me to my car. At least I was allowed to drive home.

As with the woman he had equipped with the capacity to harm me physically, I was to discover later that day why I had this huge fine. He used to take my car to get himself to and from work. I lived 60kms out of town and it was easier for him to take the car and me to get a lift to work with one of my neighbours. Then while he was working his shifts, he used to let his friends gallivant around Doha in my car. When I later received the breakdown of times and locations where these fines had been accumulated there was no way I was even in the vicinity, let alone be driving through red lights.

I woke up at 6am on the 4th of March and went to the bathroom. I had had a very restless night with pain shooting through my legs. As I stood to go to the bathroom my waters broke, and they were brown. I rushed the kids out the door to get them to school and told him we needed to get to the hospital, and we needed to get there quickly. I was taken into emergency in a wheelchair. The doctor examined me and shouted at me for not coming in earlier. Why was there no file on this pregnancy? What had I been thinking? The truth was that I was absolutely terrified, but now was not the time or place to be explaining this crazy situation that I had entangled myself into.

I am not sure how I got to the next room. All I remember is being on a big plastic covered bed where I was strapped to machines and handed a mask that I could put over my nose and mouth whenever I felt pain.

In Qatar only women are permitted to go into the delivery room. My incredible birth partner, mother of five children stood stoically as I kept falling asleep in between contractions.

Finally, after about six hours the female doctor came to me and said she wanted to perform a caesarean. After the incredible pain I had endured after Marley's Caesarean, I had been very clear that I had not wanted to have another, however in the hazy fog of whatever drugs they were pumping into me, I simply nodded my head in agreement and said to the doctor," Please tie my tubes at the same time as the caesarean."

For Marley's caesarean I had been fully knocked out. He was breach and I was not in any way ready to endure pain, so I had opted for a full anesthetic. With Amalia I only had an epidural, which meant I could feel the squelching around inside my guts as they freed this baby from the confines of the last nine months. I remember a lovely, kind-hearted man, the anesthetist I think, who sat on my side of the screen, holding my hand, reassuring me that everything was going just fine...well fine is a subjective matter of opinion.

Amalia was carried up to my head while they stitched the seven layers of my insides shut. From the first moment she was the most exquisite child. Weighing 4.5kgs it was like she was born fully formed. Her face was perfectly proportioned; thick black hair contrasting to her almost translucent skin, almond-coloured eyes, her look was quite mesmerizing. She was taken to meet her father and I was taken to a recovery ward.

Little did I know that the birth of Amalia was to be the beginning of the biggest amount of hell I think I had ever faced in my life. After three days, the hospital sent us home. I was in excruciating pain and had to be taken to the car in a wheelchair. His friend helped me into my car as he held the baby, and we were driven just a few minutes down the road to our house. Champagne glasses were raised and then I managed to make it to the first floor of the house where a bed had been made up for me next to the living room and where I would remain for the next six weeks outside of hospital appointments.

His sister was living with us at the time and had been doing an amazing job with the children. She had limited opportunities in Kenya and with two young children of her own to care for, I had offered her the opportunity to come to Qatar on a maid visa. She could live with us and run my employment agency as well as pick up work for other families, earning about ten times what she had been earning in Kenya.

My body leaked or swelled from areas I didn't know was possible. And I was absolutely starving. I asked them to bring me some food and was given the response that the house was empty of food. Having had access to a car, shops, and cash for the entire time I was in hospital, this was frustrating and somewhat unexpected on my part. He decided he could not leave the baby or me alone for even a second and as his sister could not drive, he called a friend to come and drive her to the shops.

The friend showed up about seven hours later as he was working and lived 60kms away. By this time, I was absolutely beside myself. The pain that riddled my body was exacerbated by the lack of nourishment and this was impacting my overall mental well-being. I could not understand when a shop was only two minutes away and he could have even gone out to buy take away, that he insisted on sitting over me and seemingly enjoying the torture he was putting me through. As evening fell and I had eaten nothing for around six hours the anger in me rose to uncontrollable levels. I started shouting at him that I was desperate for food and that he needed to go and buy something, anything. He, using his well formulated crazy making conversation said I would need to wait and that his friend would arrive soon and drive his sister to the supermarket. To this I picked up the remote that was sitting next to me and threw it hard and accurately at the flat screen television, smashing the screen to pieces. And now not only was I hungry and in pain, but I was also, as declared by him, a completely unreasonable crazy person. Again, he was not ignited to get some food. Instead, he went through my phone, got a number for my dear Australian friend, and called her to come over to the house immediately.

As she came into the room, I completely broke down sobbing in absolute desperation, the pain of my wound excruciating as the sobs heaved out of my body. She looked at the television and the glass all over the floor, she looked at him and his rant began. He proceeded to spew copious amounts of verbal diarrhea about how crazy I was and look what I had done to the television. The knockout of this round was mind-spinningly crazy. I could not understand the insanity and the destruction. I calmed myself and explained to my friend the situation of not having eaten since I had come out of hospital, the swelling of my breasts and the humiliation of my behaviour. Within minutes she was back to the house with cabbage leaves to soothe my breasts and food to nourish my body. His friend had showed up to take his sister shopping and instead of ever going, he disappeared with his friend...how on earth could he stay in a house full of crazy people? And returned a few days later.

My recovery was very slow, as it had been with the birth of Marley. After all I was 43 years old and more so had a very low pain threshold. After the no food incident, I had another amazing friend who put the word out amongst my work colleagues that things were not easy in my house at the moment and they organized a food roster, where every day an amazing person would bring a home-made meal to my house for us for dinner. This was not only about food, but it was also about the selfless giving and sense of community that is such a beautiful part of living in a small community. However, this act of kindness exacerbated his cruelty. He could never cope with not being the center of attention and whenever he found himself not in that position, he would pivot events to make sure he was.

When Amalia was three weeks old, and I was in the middle of healing my physical and emotional wound he decided he would take me out for a drive. I can't remember whether we were going to the shops or just a drive. I had thought after everything it would be nice to be together just the two of us and agreed that this was a great idea. As we left the compound gates an argument was already cooked up. Yet another of his crazy making scenarios where I would constantly try to make sense of something that was senseless. Where I would justify and defend my position only to feed him more power to twist and feed his narcissistic mind. We were only one roundabout into the journey, and he was already furious. By the second roundabout he decided to accelerate and keep driving round the circle of the roundabout, throwing my fragile body towards the interior side of the door. As I clutched the upper handle with one hand and the wound in my stomach with the other, I could feel the tearing of the wound. I screamed in pain, asking him to stop, telling him to take me home. In the space of less than ten minutes I was literally thrown out of the car on my doorstep, the kids coming out to see what had happened, me in a curled sobbing heap on the ground, clutching my stomach, my head spinning.

The next day he left for Kenya. Amalia was three weeks old. Of course, he didn't tell me he was going. He had told his sister. That was all he needed to do. He had to go and visit his kids. He had other kids you know, and he needed to be there to take care of them, not just this one...he had others! This verse was one that I would hear hundreds of times over the course and beyond our relationship.

The nurses arrived at 11am as they always did to monitor and clean my wound. As they removed the gauze they recoiled in shock. The wound that had been healing so perfectly was now a decimated mess. It was open, leaking, and infected. As they asked what had happened, heavy tears just rolled down my cheeks. They were respectful enough not to ask further questions. They prescribed a course of antibiotics and checked their schedule to see if they could fit me in more often than once a week. They knew I needed to be monitored.

In Qatar you only get six weeks maternity leave. You receive an hour a day to go and feed your baby and if strategically planned this can work well into the day. I knew I was not physically ready to go back to work; however, I could not get the female doctor to give me a medical certificate to stay off longer. The day before I was to return to work, his sister walked out of our house, never to return. She moved in with one of my neighbours and never spoke to either myself or any of my children, including Amalia again. She was my full-time care giver of Amalia while I was at work. There was no way he was going to stay at home to take care of a child, despite the fact that he earned a tenth of what I earned and so Tashania had to stop going to school and stay at home to look after the baby while I went to work.

While this may sound harsh, Qatar has some very unique rules when you live and work there and basically if I did not go to work, none of us would have anywhere to live. We were totally in damage control on every level, so this was the best I could do. It was like a hornet's nest and all I was doing was attracting crap. The carer had walked out; I was juggling how we were going to get out of this country. Trying to get Amalia a Qatari residency permit, knowing that in the next month the children and I would be homeless if my employer kicked us out of the company house, that my accounts would be frozen and that it was going to be at the height of a Middle Eastern summer with temperatures rising to a steady 50 degrees, 70 percent humidity and dust storms so fierce you were in a constant state of exfoliant.

That summer we had our first date in court. The way I knew I had to present myself in court was because someone had told me I should go to the courthouse and ask them to tell me when my date was. Hmm! And if I had not known to go to the courthouse? Absolutely everything inside this building was in Arabic and was predominantly all male. Remember that I had not actually committed a crime and was being held inside this country for the mere act of having lost my job while having a bank loan. As I walked into the crowed courthouse, I found a kind person, who found my letter and translated it for me, telling me that my date was just a couple of days away. Thank God I had gone to check! I had been advised to show up to court with the children. This was to be a bit of a mercy card. So, I prepared myself in my beautiful full length black abaya, got the children ready with lunchboxes, nappies, and copious amounts of drinking water and drove through the heat to the courthouse. As we positioned ourselves on a wooden bench inside the room, the kids started opening their food and eating. At this point a man came and promptly escorted us out to a waiting area. I would be called when it was my turn.

I walked in not long after and was escorted to the front of the room, past benches full of Arabic speaking men. There were three men seated high behind a wooden bench wearing their traditional white robes and head dress. I knew there had to be a rational outcome to this irrational situation. The judge would either dissolve the loan and let me leave or tell my employer they needed to reinstate me so I could pay off the loan. I don't speak Arabic, did not have a lawyer, as I had not committed a crime and not a word was spoken in English. So, when the guy in white stopped talking, I was simply escorted out and told to go home. And this was the routine for the numerous amounts of court appearances I was to have over the following few months. I had no idea what was going on.

I managed to secure a teaching job in a school in Doha to begin in September of 2014. They knew about my situation, but as the term was just about to begin, they must have been desperate. I would teach Grade 6 and Aaliyah would be in my class. Marley started his traumatic educational journey in Reception at this school and Tashania was still staying at home to take care of Amalia.

Living in Doha with him was an absolute nightmare. Now his hyena style antics had free range. When I had lived sixty kilometers away from the nearest city, he was forced to be less distracted from the city lights, but now we were in Doha he had everything he wanted. He would come and go from the house as he pleased. Nobody would know when he would be there or when he would be sleeping somewhere else. Perhaps his work accommodation, perhaps not.

I was tired. I had a class of crazy children, predominantly Arabic boys, who were rich and unmotivated by the understandable boredom of a curriculum that offered them very little apart from the acquisition of English for their future. I still had a court case, no house help to take care of Amalia, and Marley absolutely hating going to school. My account was still frozen, so I had no money, the house we had moved into was overflowing with boxes and I was breast feeding a four-month-old baby.

I was really tired! He came in one night after yet another of his all too familiar prowling escapades. He was wearing his work uniform and I cannot remember if he was drunk or not. I had this bed that I really loved. Made from Omani wood it was a heavy set wooden, Arabic style four poster bed with white mosquito netting flowing from the railings. The bedside light was on, and I was feeding Amalia. As he came into the bedroom, my tiredness leapt up and I started questioning him on his latest disappearance. This was something it took me a very long time to give up on. Questioning. I learned the lesson the hard way; narcissists don't ever take kindly to being asked or expected to answer questions. He removed his belt and the next thing I knew my bare legs were covered in the welts of the leather slapping and cutting into them. But I was tired! So very tired! The tears from my face dropped down onto his daughter as I sheltered her body with my free arm from this flying leather strap. Eventually he went to shower. I removed this innocent child from my breast and carefully placed her into her cot. Then I rolled into my all too familiar fetal position and pretended to be asleep, least he come back.

Early December of 2014, my employer called me into the office and gleefully told me that I had not passed probation. They did not feel I had the best interests of the children at heart. As I explained my own child was in the class, so how could I possibly not have the best interests of the children at the forefront of my teaching. Nevertheless, I was told not to come back in January. Knockout! No school for the children and facing homelessness again, in a Middle Eastern country with rules that were so crazy I don't think even they themselves could have made sense of them if they had tried.

On the 31st of December 2014 I put three of my children on a one-way ticket back to their father in Melbourne. On the 25th of December, the children and I had spent Christmas together in the park. Mr. Rwanda hated any sort of celebration that did not focus around him, because he could not stand for anyone else to have any attention their way thus detracting from it being aimed towards him. And it even applied to Jesus! He left the house very early, not caring to spend any time with his new daughter on her first Christmas.

With the three other children in Australia, I had to set about packing and moving out of yet another house. Amalia and I were going to stay with a dear friend who offered her kindness to us and for which we are eternally indebted. However, I still needed some cash flow.

I got a message from a friend saying I should apply for a job he had seen advertised online asking for an English Language Teacher. There were not too many details, but I applied, had the interview, and was offered the position. It was a position teaching English to one of the senior members of the Royal family. I was given an entry permit for multiple palaces where the lessons would be held. I would sit at tables frequented by Presidents and would teach English. One day I was told my student needed to learn the English vocabulary required to describe jewellery. My student had specific clothing and jewellery designers who would fly in from all over the world to meet with her and discuss the specifications of her jewellery requirements. She told me she would bring some catalogues to our next class.

The table was large enough for about twenty people. I arrived expecting to see catalogues similar to IKEA but with jewellery. Instead, I found leather bound, gold embossed folders, so heavy, filled with exquisite glossy photographs of jewellery I had never seen before. And so, I taught the lesson. I taught the names of all the precious stones, the embellishments, the crusting and all the other vocabulary required when meeting with an Italian jewellery designer who would charge a million dollars for a necklace and some matching earrings...and all the while I was trapped inside this country without any ability to get out and be with my children until the court case was completed.

I called my dad...things were bad! The court case was going nowhere and every time I appeared it just drew out more time. I started meeting people who were in the same situation as me. Some of them had been in Qatar for ten years and many were from extremely low-income backgrounds where their initial loan may have only been a few hundred dollars. It was such a systemic issue, based on laws that were outdated and to my knowledge have changed slightly since my time. When I called dad, I was actually asking him to help me come up with some sort of a solution. I was not exactly sure what that solution would be. Possibly that stereotypical model of getting local or Federal government in Australia involved, alerting the media of my plight, the fact that three of my children were in Australia and I could not join them and the one who was with me was now considered illegal in Qatar. Dad sent me the money and bailed me out around forty thousand dollars. Onward and upward...or so I thought. I had already accepted what I thought was my dream job in Rwanda. Mr. Rwanda was not coming. He was keeping his job in Qatar and was going to escort Amalia and I to the country of his father's birth and then return to Qatar and keep working.

However, Amalia had been born in a country where the labor laws required the parents to have a job where the employer would write a sponsorship letter for the baby to get a residency permit for the country she was born in, so she could leave and go to the country her grandfather had been born in. That long paragraph without punctuation was deliberately written to highlight yet another insanity of my situation. So, I could leave Qatar, however Amalia who was not yet a year old could not. Amalia has a Qatari birth certificate; however, she needed a residency permit in order to exit the country. I was unemployed and while I begged my former employer, whose permit I was still under, to write the letter, confusion and insanity was the name of the game and they refused. Her father did not earn a high enough salary to have his employer write the letter and yet another game of cat and mouse played out.

In the heat of summer, Amalia and I made multiple trips to the old immigration office in Doha to see if we could get this matter sorted. I met many Abdullahs and the same number of Muhammeds. None of them could understand why my husband could not sponsor the baby. They would look at my papers, tell me to get my husband to sponsor the child and move on to the next customer pushing others out of their way to get the attention of the officer.

After more visits than I care to remember I finally found a kind-hearted senior officer who understood English fluently and who offered to assist me in my plight. He issued Amalia with a visit visa and as I literally fell over with sheer joy, I thought all my problems had been solved and I would soon be on my way. All I had to do now was go and have my residency permit cancelled and Amalia and I would be on our way to my dream job in my dream country.

Another 'final' visit to immigration would mean we would be good to go. I would have my permit cancelled, we could book our flight and leave the following day...or so I thought. In order to have one's residency cancelled the sponsor 'me' needed to have no liabilities under their sponsorship. This included things like a car, boat, housemaid and...anyone on a tourist visa.

The immigration officer explained it so simply...madam the person on the tourist visa just needs to exit the country before you. Then you come back to immigration once that person has left and we will cancel your visa and you can leave...but the person on the tourist visa was not yet one year old, had been born in this country and was travelling out with her mother (me!).

We got it all sorted and one month before Amalia turned one year old, we were living in Rwanda.

Love Susan

TEA WITH KILLERS

April 2015,

Kigali, Rwanda

> "Better to die fighting for freedom than be a prisoner all the
> days of your life." Bob Marley.

Dear Mum

Rwanda taught me many life-changing lessons. One of the most
confronting and eye opening has been about killers! The killers
who I have shared dinner with, the killers who I have shared
coffee with and the killers whose children play with mine. The
thing that I continue to wonder is whether or not these people
are actually killers, or is it just a matter of perspective? Is there
are difference between a killer and a liberator? There is a
historical perspective in many parts of Africa that through liter-
ature leads the reader to believe that a person who led his
country to independence is a freedom fighter. For a person
such as me, it is not my place to judge whether a person is a

freedom fighter or a killer, or whether they are killing to liberate or propagate. In fact, many of the people who were once called Freedom Fighters in Colonial Africa, would now be referred to as terrorists.

So, when you greet someone with a handshake, do you think about the fact that it is the same hand that has taken a gun and shot another human being through the heart? Or do you just shake their hand and get on with enjoying the moment of the children playing together or the tea you are about to pour from the tea pot?

It's a weird experience when you sit down and discover that if a person was in the army, then they have probably taken the life of another person. In Australia, it is not like that. In Australia, you can be in the army and never see a battle. In Rwanda, if you are in the army and of a certain age, the probability of having faced the atrocities of war are very high. Here people joined the army specifically to liberate their country. They will do whatever it takes to achieve that goal. A country that they may not have been born in, but a country that they are proud to call their home. The fact that they were not born here is another reason that fuelled them to join the army. For if they had been provided with the liberty of permission to have been born here then there would have been no need to liberate.

One of the things that were so shocking to face in Rwanda was the sheer brutality of the killing that took place during the genocide. Just before we left, we visited one of the many sites that had been turned into a memorial/ education facility. The site was a church. More than ten thousand people had sought refuge inside the church in 1994 and all of them had been brutally massacred. The word brutal may actually not even be the right adjective to describe what some of these people endured. Inside the memorial the bones of those who were massacred lay scattered. Skulls had been smashed through with a machete. The bodies of pregnant women who had been ripped in half. Thousands of pieces of individual bones that had been dismembered from their owner's bodies.

This letter is one that has been really difficult for me to complete. I have sat with it for years, knowing it is not politically correct yet also knowing it has been one of my biggest learning experiences. In yoga we are taught to be a silent witness. To surrender judgement. This does not mean condoning behaviours, nor does it mean taking sides. To me the silent witness means standing in the present moment. Observing why you drew that moment into your life and enjoying the hot, sweet taste of the tea.

Love Susan

IN MY FACE

25th of February 2016

Kigali, Rwanda

"Your penis betrayed you son." Richard Brautigan

Dear Mum

It was late and dark. I liked to sleep with the curtains open. My room was on the top floor and with the curtains open you could see the lights shining like stars across the hills of Kigali. His penis was hovering over my face, He wanted to urinate on me. "You are a Genocidaire! That is why you got fired! That is why all these things are happening to you in Rwanda!" Was I dreaming? Most people in the world that I come from would not even know what a Genocidaire is. "You are a Hutu supporter! You are anti-government! That is why you got fired from your job!" I rubbed my eyes. Not daring to push that penis out of my face for fear of further repercussions. How could I possibly be a Genocidaire? A Genocidaire is a supporter of the

Tutsi massacre in the Genocide of 1994. Rwanda today is filled with prisons of such people who have been convicted of atrocities committed during the 100-day massacre. In 1994 I was living a comfortable life in Kenya. As my life continued, I had a child with a Tutsi. How could I possibly be a Genocidaire? I loved this country more than any other. The progressive government and forward-thinking policies were an example to the rest of Africa and in a lot of cases to the world. He put his penis away, but it would be removed and placed strategically in my face twice again that night in an attempt to urinate on me.

I woke up! That was not a dream that was a nightmare!

When I first moved to Rwanda, I felt like there were literally skeletons everywhere. I would hear trucks rumbling past my house at night and have flashbacks to the news clips and movies that had been prevalent around 1994. But Rwanda is one of the most amazing examples of hope and reconciliation that the world has ever seen. The roads are smooth and paved all the way out to the countryside. There are no potholes that are all too familiar in Kenya and other African countries. To buy milk we walk to our local milk zone with our refillable container and have it filled to the quantity of our liking. Plastic bags are banned throughout the country and if you are caught entering the airport with plastic it is confiscated. Seventy per cent of the government is made up of women. This is a country that certainly holds a lot of progressive ideologies that in many cases cannot be compared to anywhere else in the world.

Sending lots of love

Susan

NIGHTMARES

26th of February 2016

Kigali, Rwanda

"Can a person who feels unlovable bear to be loved?" ACIM

Dear Mum

There is something quite unique about an African sky at night. In my younger days I loved taking a train from Nairobi to Mombasa. It was an overnight train and in the middle of the night the train would travel through Tsavo National Park. The blanket of stars that engulfed the sky was truly an incredible sight. I would sit at the back of the open train and drink those stars into my being. Likewise sitting by a campfire in the Masai Mara, introducing the local Masai security guards to toasted marshmallows while the sounds of wild animals could be heard echoing in the night sky. The light of the Masai torches combined with the light of the stars creating shadows that we thought could be leopards walking into the campsite. The laughter of the hyenas in the distance sending chills down our spines. On those nights we were not allowed to even walk alone to the toilet in the campsite. Should you need to make that journey, you would have to do so escorted by one of the Masai guards. In Rwanda, the beauty that night holds are breathtaking. Being the Land of a Thousand Hills, the city of Kigali twinkles like a star filled sky. Power blackouts in Kigali are an all-too-common affair. On these nights, the hills stretching out across from my house would be pitch black. The only light to be seen were the stars above and the headlights of cars passing on the winding roads through the hills.

I woke with a start at 3am one night. His backhand knocked me to the ground as I opened the door to let him in. 'You whore...I fucking hate you!' another backhand knocked me down as I tried to pull myself closer to the now locked front door of the house. With blood running down my nose, he climbed on top of me. Forcing me to do things I didn't want to do. I lay there telling him I loved him...telling him not to hurt me...telling him that he was the most important person in my world...

An African night sky is so powerful. That night, I thought I was going to die. Who would even know? I was inside this house, inside a country that was not mine. I sat bolt upright. Rubbing my eyes, becoming conscious again, I could see that the bed sheets were wet from my perspiration and the pillows had been thrown to the floor. Why was I having such nightmares?

The nightmares came think and fast during that year I spent in Rwanda. On another night I was being whipped with a cable. Lashes cracked across the skin of my back, legs, and arms. I curled myself into the tiniest of balls in an attempt to soften the blows. Finally, the lashing stopped, and he left. Where he went, I will never know. In fact, where he went, I will never care.

I still don't have any answers or explanations for the horrific nightmares I suffered when I was living in Rwanda. But when I left...they stopped.

Susan

BLOOD OR DEATH?

Date of events unknown:

"Manipulation is a contagious disease, much more dangerous that the flu because it can endure for a lifetime." Dorothy Mccoy

Dear Mum

This was now the million-dollar question...although deep within me I already knew what the answer was! I felt as though I had invested my entire life into the love of this one person. I believed that if I loved him enough, everything would be OK. That we would have our happily ever after and that we would live together as a family!

But as time went on and his cunning ways and streetwise use of manipulation enabled him to adjust his abuse to different cultural settings and international laws, things did not improve. In fact, things got worse! So, I had to stop and breathe and reflect on the question above. I knew a reasonable amount of his past. I remember a story he told with so much pride to anyone who had the time to listen. In fact, it was not only he who would tell the story. Other family members would also retell how he had acted during a time of tragedy.

It was a normal Nairobi day and the woman who had raised him was crossing the street in front of her house to purchase some items from the market. She was getting on in age, however, was still too young to die, even in Africa where life expectancy is less than many Western countries.

From out of nowhere came a bicycle. Not a motorcycle, or a car, a bicycle, ridden by a young man who may not have eaten that day and was on his was to earn some form of income to put food on the table for his loved ones.

As she was knocked, her long, frail body fell onto the potholed road. An ambulance would be political and would take too long, so a good Samaritan put her bleeding body into his car, and she was rushed to hospital.

The only way the old woman had a chance of survival was if she was given a blood transfusion. She had given birth to many children who themselves had grown children of their own. Unfortunately for her, he was the only one who had the same blood type.

He was contacted. However, he had no love for this woman. It appeared he had no inkling of a feeling at all. Despite the fact that she had raised him albeit not so well, but she did what she could under the circumstances.

They begged and they cried to him through the phone receiver and possibly as he had done to me more times than I could ever count, he hung up the call and refused to pick the multitude of frantic calls that continued through the state of sheer desperation to save the life of this woman.

And then she died...

I met him many years after she died, and he never once showed remorse for his actions. He would shamelessly tell this story to people who were willing to give him an ear and he never seemed to sense that his behaviour was not acceptable. For there was nothing stopping him from donating blood to save her life, apart from his ego.

Love Susan

FOOT IN MOUTH

April 2015, Kigali, Rwanda

"Be careful with your words. Once they are said they can only
be forgiven, not forgotten." Unknown.

Dear Mum

When one lives abroad, the opportunity for foot in mouth
disease strikes you on an all too regular basis. The powers in
play, that being the cultural idiosyncrasies that always strike at
the forefront of cross-cultural encounters seem to come up at
the worst moments.

I had been working in Kigali for a few months. I had two of the
loveliest secretaries, who had assisted me with every aspect of
settling into the job. We talked a lot, but as the workload was so
demanding, we never really had time to get to know each other.
One early morning the younger of the two ladies came into the
office to do some pre-work preparations. She was about twenty-
three years old at the time. I said to her very casually "So do

you live with your parents?" She replied that she did not. I continued the conversation by asking what her parents did. She replied telling me that they were 'digging for gold." Being Australian and reasonably familiar with gold mining, I excitedly exclaimed that that was great. Where did they do this gold, digging was my next question. She looked at me with her sweet smile and said "They are dead! They had been killed in the genocide when she was two years old!" My jaw dropped as I froze at the computer I was sitting at, feeling completely ashamed at the fact that I had responded excitedly. With mortal embarrassment I apologized and explained what digging for gold meant in my world. I honestly thought her parents were working on a gold mine in Congo.

In actual fact they had both been killed in front of her eyes as she hid under a bed in their family home. The killers had not heard her suppressed crying and she had escaped death. For the next twenty years of her life, she grew up with various relatives. She, like many Rwandans who had experienced such atrocities, was incredibly resilient and certainly not a victim of her situation. She has educated herself to a college level, found herself a good job and supported herself financially. In this instant my foot in mouth did not cause any offence and proved to be the learning of an eternally humbling story for me.

Another instance, also in Rwanda and also with my secretary was just after memorial week. The 7th of April 1994 was the day the President of Rwanda and Burundi's plane was shot down, triggering the start of the 100-day massacre. Every year the country closes down for a week of reflection and remembrance. Just after work resumed, my secretary came into work wearing a black T-shirt. On the front was a circular emblem with people standing inside it. I commented to her that I really liked her T-shirt. She replied saying that all the people on the

T-shirt were her family members who had been killed in the genocide. I just wanted the earth to open there and then and swallow me up. How can you even offer and apology? Again, she was extremely humble by my foot in mouth and again I was extremely grateful for that.

Foot in mouth disease can be endemic when you are living in another culture. I remember when two of my friends came to visit me in Kenya from Australia. They were both quite large ladies at the time and as we were sitting around the dinner table one night, I commented that African men like big women. One of the two replied "well we will be ok then!" To which Mr. Kenya stated "No! You guys are just too big!" As I slunk under the table dying of embarrassment my friends luckily took this as an example of foot in mouth.

In Kenya it was very common to be called 'fat' as a compliment. My mother-in-law once said to me "Susan, you sure are looking fat today!" That example of foot in mouth was enough for me to stop eating for about a week. From a culture where to be fat was a complete social taboo, to one where to be fat meant that you were well fed and thus healthy. Many Africans in those days had grown up where food was scarce. Therefore, to be thin meant you were unhealthy and underfed.

The number of times that I have encountered foot in mouth disease is too many to count. Sometimes you end up laughing, but most of the time the disease leads to tears and often heartbreak.

Lots of love Susan

BUSES, BABIES AND BORDERS

March 2016,

Kigali, Rwanda, Kampala, Uganda

Dear Mum

The task of the leader is to get his people from where they are to where they have not been. ~ Henry Kissinger

Buses, Babies and Borders! Friday the 4th of March 2016. Amalia's second birthday. We had arrived in Rwanda just over a year prior, by plane from Qatar. Due to our struggling state of financial affairs, we were leaving Rwanda by bus on what was to be a grueling thirty something hours of travelling by road across three countries to Kenya.

Tears streamed down my cheeks as the bus rolled along through the winding hills of Rwanda towards the Ugandan border. The cascading hills that housed rice paddies resembling those of Vietnam. Tea plantations that sat in the valleys were something I had never seen before. The scenery reflected the eternal beauty of Rwanda. I posted on Facebook that falling in love with a country was like falling in love with a man. You leave your heart open to be broken. Now it was that with my heart shattered into a thousand pieces, the country that I loved so much was passing into the distance behind me.

Bob Marley played my all-time favorite Redemption Song through my headphones. "Those pirates yes they rob us." Even though I knew that bigger and better things were waiting for me, these pirates, the school I had worked for, had robbed me. They had robbed me of the experience I had gone to Rwanda to have. They had robbed my daughter of being in her homeland. Of speaking her mother tongue fluently. However, I think there is something that a thief is unaware of. When something is robbed from you, it is simply exchanged for something that is given. While I perceived that Amalia and I had been robbed of Rwanda, perhaps what we were to be given as a result of the robbery was of far more importance. Amalia got the physical presence of her father back. He had been told of the difficulties we were facing in Rwanda and returned to assist us with all aspects of the mess we were in. He sorted our visas, helped us move to a new house, and attended meetings with the lawyer we were using to achieve justice from the school, transported our belongings out of Rwanda and escorted us on this journey across borders. Most importantly for me, he was there to light the candles on her birthday cake and to tuck her into bed at night. Having been separated from him for four months, she was not keen to let him out of her sight, even for one minute. The robbery had in fact given her back her dad.

"Emancipate yourselves from mental slavery, none but our selves can free our minds." That was all I had tried to do through my position of leadership in that school. In fact, it is what I do through any leadership position I am in. Emancipate! As the Acting Primary School Principal, I helped serve rice with the kitchen team to over seven hundred children and their teachers. This act was not about serving rice. It was about building bonds with people. It was about teamwork and valuing people and the roles they play in the overall functioning of the organization and thus in the lives of the people. It was about getting to know the stories of the staff, showing unity and respect.

I had brought a vision of hope to a downtrodden group of teachers who had worked under oppressive working conditions. I had built bridges; I had instilled a sense of value, of respect and of unity. But most importantly I had taught people to believe in themselves. So, you know what Bob Marley? You are right. People do need to emancipate themselves from mental slavery and you are right that none but ourselves can free our minds. However, sometimes people need a little push in the right direction to firstly see that they are not emancipated and then to adjust their minds accordingly.

When I had first started in the school, I had identified a need to strengthen the middle leadership team. I had asked the team of eight three questions: What do we do well, what do we need to improve on, and what can I do for you? The third question was one the team had never been asked before. The common thread to all eight answers was that I can listen to them. Done! I am very good at listening. And as time went on, I listened. Just like serving rice in the kitchen, this act was about valuing people, about showing respect, about emancipating.

So, the management fired me! Again Bob Marley, you are right: "But my hand was made strong, by the hand of the almighty!" Insecure managers do not want their teams to be emancipated. Insecure managers want their teams to remain under their control. The control of a one-year contract, so you cannot even take a loan to build a house. The control of a low wage that keeps you indebted to them just so your children receive a semi-decent education. The control of hiring and firing at whim without any regard to the fact that the individual has financial and physical commitments that are dependent on that low wage.

For me, the hand of the almighty created me to be strong. I would not be a victim of this situation and the people that I cared about inside the system would also not be subjected to this lack of emancipation for their entire careers. Justice would be achieved. As we left Rwanda and crossed the border into Uganda however, we were not sure what form that justice would take.

So, the bus journey continued. At the exact time of her birth two years earlier, Amalia left the country of her grandfather's birth and crossed into Uganda.

Thinking of you all

Susan

HELD HOSTAGE

July 7th, 1996, Nairobi, Kenya.

"Everything that feels suffocating teaches us how to breathe."
Mandy Antoniacci

Dear Mum

I was tear gassed inside a bank in Nairobi, the capital city of Kenya. It was around the time of the very famous saba saba in Kenya. Saba, saba means seventh of the seventh. It was a time of great political turmoil in Kenya and as each subsequent year passed, tensions rose across the city. A group of friends and I had arranged to spend this particular weekend out of Nairobi. We were to meet at the bank on the corner of Moi and Kenyatta Ave, right in the center of Nairobi. The working hours of the bank on a Saturday were half day, so after my friends had finished, we planned to get a matatu (public bus) and head off on the three-hour journey to our destination. I must have arrived at the bank at around 12:30pm. Walked into the banking hall and sat down waiting for my friends to finish work. Within minutes there was the sound of gunshots being fired outside the bank. I had never even heard gunshots before, but there is something inside you that automatically tells you things are not alright. The huge wooden doors of the banking hall were rapidly padlocked shut and those remaining inside buckled down and waited to see what would happen next. A group of us went up to the first floor and saw that there were cars all over the streets below, possibly with plain clothed policemen inside. Whoever they were they were carrying huge guns that were resting on the open windows ready to fire.

As the hours went on people started relaxing and chatting away to pass the time. In those days there were no mobile phones. All the internal phone lines were down and there was no way of contacting people outside the city center. After about four hours there was a barrage of police outside and suddenly the entire bank was filled with the most toxic smelling fumes one could imagine. We all lay down on the floor and covered our faces with whatever we could find. The smoke was intoxicating! Tears were streaming down my cheeks and my throat was constricted beyond belief. With the smoke engulfing the entire bank, we were totally trapped. We could not leave the bank for fear of being shot.

After about six hours we managed to get a call out of the bank on the old-style landlines they had in Kenya at the time. We called a friend who also worked in the bank but had left work early that Saturday thus avoiding all the chaos we were experiencing inside. He had a car. An old-style Peugeot 504 and wanted to see if he could get into town, collect us, and take us safely out of the city center.

Behind the bank there was a narrow laneway that connected to a small back entrance. About an hour later there was a loud knock on the door. It was opened carefully and there was our friend waiting to escort us out of there. Ten of us piled into the car, crouching down so as not to be seen. The driver drove quickly through the city centre, and we were out of the CBD within a few minutes. To my surprise on the outskirts of town, life was continuing as normal. Matatus were plying their regular routes, women were selling fruit and vegetables on the side of the road and people were going about their daily business completely unaware of what I had been through inside the bank that afternoon.

We got to the matatu stand where the matatus left for our upcountry destination. I was so surprised to hear that my friends were still planning on partaking in our weekend away. I was so traumatized from the day's activities that I said I would just go home, and they should go on ahead of me. That idea was one they were not entertaining at all. Reluctantly I piled into the matatu with the others and our long journey out of town began.

The other members of my party did not seem particularly affected by the morning's tear gas or shootings in the bank. They sang and talked happily as I rested my head on the seat in front of me. We travelled for about two hours. It was now very dark. The roads were windy and potholed and the journey extremely uncomfortable. All of a sudden, our matau stopped. I felt like we were in the middle of nowhere. He told us we all needed to get out of the vehicle. He had reached his destination and was not interested in taking us any further. Oh my! Could this day possibly get any worse? Now we were left stranded in the middle of a dark road in the middle of nowhere with no means of reaching our destination.

I have learnt over the years that it is important not to get stressed in such a situation. Stress only causes internal and external conflict and doesn't ever help a situation. I have also learnt that tough situations always get resolved somehow. As it so happens, another matatu passed by about an hour later. By pure coincidence, this matatu was heading in our direction and had just enough seats to accommodate our entire group. We made it! I collapsed into bed and think I slept for about two days!

Sending lots of love

Susan

AFRICAN BABY GIRL

September 1997, Nairobi, Kenya

"The love of a parent for a child is the love that should grow
towards separation." Khalil Gibran

Dear Mum

One of my childhood dreams was to adopt an African baby girl.
I knew it had to be a girl because I had always been so fascinated with their hair. Little did I know at the time that that hair
would become a lifelong learning experience for me!

I had heard about New Life Home, which at the time was situ-
ated in the suburb of Loresho, about eight kilometers outside
Nairobi on the Naivasha Road.

At the time of my first visit to the home I was single. On a
bright Saturday afternoon, a friend and I decided we would go
to the home, have a look around and get some information.

After signing in the askari opened the gates and we were greeted by two beautiful Golden Retrievers. We walked inside and there were babies everywhere. Babies in bouncers on the floor, babies hanging from swings in doorways, babies being fed by nurses and volunteers and babies scooting around in walkers.

Through the sea of babies, we saw Clive and Mary Beckingham. A British couple in their mid-fifties, Clive and Mary had come to Kenya and started this home for HIV positive and abandoned babies. The couple had grown up children of their own and had adopted a son of their own from the home.

Clive and Mary along with their research team had discovered that babies who were born HIV positive, but who had never been breastfed, had a high probability of reversing their HIV status to negative. After which these babies could only contract HIV in the same way as anybody else.

At this time New Life Home was quite a small organization. Since then, it has moved to a much larger premise in Hurlingham, has many more selfless nurses and volunteers and has opened branches in other areas of Kenya that have been particularly hard hit by HIV.

Consequently, on the day we went, Clive and Mary had time to sit down with us, offer us a cup of coffee and talk us through the procedure of adoption in Kenya.

Basically, at that time, Kenya had relatively few restrictions for adopting babies to anyone who was a Kenyan resident. You could be single, married, African or foreign. There simply were too many babies and not enough good families wanting to adopt them.

The home required that after choosing your baby, the prospective parents would visit them three times while they were still in the home. During this time, you could feed, play with and bond with the child. Assuming that all went well, you could then take your baby home. There was then a three-month fostering period set by the Kenyan government. During this time, a social worker would come to your house to do a home study report and check that bonding was going well, and that the child was now a settled member of the family. This was also the time when all documentation would be prepared for court. After the court hearing, the new parents would get a birth certificate with your name as the parents and the name you had chosen for the child and the baby would be legally yours.

Driving back to Nairobi that day, my head was spinning. What I had been told that I was eligible to adopt a baby from Kenya and that basically in three days I could be a mother! Now that really was too big!

Subconsciously it was about nine months later that I went back to that same home in Loresho with Mr. Kenya. Mr. Kenya and I had met shortly after my first visit to the home. We met through a mutual friend on one of their work trips to Amboseli National Park.

As many romances do, our life together started as a bit of a whirlwind and before we knew it, we were living together and talking about the prospect of adopting a baby. Africans generally hold their blood lines as being of vital importance. This is for many reasons, but predominantly due to inheritance of land. Thus, formal adoptions such as the one I wanted were not particularly common in those days. Informal adoptions, however, were very common, in the form of cousins or other blood linked relatives being raised from very young babies in the homes of relatives. Mr. Kenya himself had grown up with a cousin being raised in his family home until he was an adult.

On a bright Sunday morning at the end of September, we woke up and Mr. Kenya surprised me by suggesting that today was the day we should go home and have a look at the babies. I was not in agreement with his suggestion because I knew deep in my heart that this time it would be very difficult for me to leave without a baby of my own. In true Mr. Kenya style, he said we should just go and see what happened.

After lunch on the same day, we headed down Naivasha Road to the orphanage. It was Mr. Kenya's first time! We signed in, patted the dogs, and headed inside, where we were once again greeted by Clive and Mary. Of course, they recognized me from my previous visit and must have now understood that I was serious.

Clive and Mary gave us a full tour through the orphanage, where we entered a number of rooms filled with double decker pink or blue baby cots. Each cot had the baby's chart with their name on it posted above their bed, but Mary did not need to refer to these, as she knew the name of every child, along with the story that had brought them to be in the home.

As we walked around, one tiny baby particularly struck Mr. Kenya. She was snuggled deep beneath her blankets with her head facing down and away from us. All we could really see was this flock of brown curly hair!

After our tour, we were escorted into Clive and Mary's office. We were then asked a series of questions. Did we want a boy or a girl? How old would we prefer the child to be and what HIV status did we prefer, positive or negative? We explained that we wanted a girl who was as young as possible. As we were first time parents, we preferred a child who was HIV negative.

Mary disappeared for a few minutes and returned carrying one of only two girls they had in the home at that time. It was the tiny girl with all the hair that Mr. Kenya had spotted earlier. She had lighter skin than the other baby and Mary thought she was perfectly suited to the two of us. As I write this letter, that tiny baby is now twenty four years old, and Mary could not have been more accurate in her thoughts. Tashania is and has always been the perfect choice for us. I held this baby and instantly knew she was ours!

In those days, adopting a girl child in Kenya was generally more difficult than adopting a boy. At the time of Tashania's adoption the home only had two girls and seventeen boys. This fact was in part due to cultural reasons. If a single woman gives birth to a male child, she is led to believe that no man will marry her in the future, because he would not want to father a child who was not his blood for inheritance reasons. This is something that I believe has changed over the years and people are becoming more open minded to the idea of parenting the children of other people. A girl child on the other hand, in those days, which were born to a single mother, can be a useful source of domestic labor. Even from a young age there are many uses for a girl child within the family unit. A girl child was also not considered an obstacle for inheritance because the blood line runs through the males.

When we met Tashania her name was June. She had been named after the lady who had brought her into the home. By coincidence, her birthday was also in June. She had been born in Jamaa Nursing Home in Nairobi to a fourteen-year-old birth mother. Both the birth mother and her aunt had decided to sign the baby over for adoption, so at one day old she was taken straight to New Life Home. To my limited knowledge, the birth mother never saw her baby and it was June who collected her and brought her to New Life Home.

Poverty and desperation in many third world countries lead young women to make some of the hardest life decisions. In Kenya babies are dumped in all manner of places. No one can imagine the trauma a birth mother must endure at that moment and then for the rest of their lives. Mr. Kenya and I have nothing but respect for this child, who was Tashania's birth mother. She took a brave road of giving birth in a hospital and then signing her baby over to what she would have hoped would be a better life for her child than what she could provide.

I remember many years later when we were about to collect Aaliyah from her orphanage but due to her being ill, the nuns would not release her until the following day. Tashania who at the time was seven years old and I went to the airport to collect an Australian friend who I was working with in Qatar. Her flight had been delayed and Tashania and I decided to take a walk around the airport. As we walked along holding hands, Tashania who had now become very aware of the adoption process through our new experience of adopting Aaliyah said "mummy, whose tummy did I come out of?" I replied that the only thing I knew about the person was that she had come out of the tummy of a fourteen-year-old lady. Her only response was "That is not a lady, that's a girl!" This innate wisdom is something that has become a piece of what makes Tashania an incredible person to be around. As she has grown older, she seems to be wiser. Sometimes forcing me to forget that she is the child, and I am an adult.

There was another time when Tashania was only five years old, and we were living in Malaysia. It was a small school, but the teacher was new and not aware of our situation. In class they were learning about where babies come from and one of the mums in the class came in with her newborn. When Tashania was very small we would tell her that she came from the Baby Shop. We would take her back to Kenya frequently and we would always visit the orphanage. She would see the bed that had been hers and meet the people who had taken care of her. She would see all the other babies and think this was where babies came from.

So here in Malaysia her young teacher was explaining where babies came from to a group of five-year olds when Tashania interjected. "I didn't come from my mummy's tummy. I came from the Baby Shop!" The teacher responded by saying that all babies come from their mommy's tummy. Tashania at this point stood up and vehemently disagreed with the teacher, once again reinstating that she did not come from her mummy's tummy. She came from the Baby Shop. Later that day a perplexed teacher came to me and explained Tashania's response to the lesson on where babies come from. Backing up Tashania's point I then explained the story of how Tashania came to be a part of our lives to the teacher. That afternoon I had to explain to Tashania that for many people their mother is the person whose tummy they came out of, but not always.

So, I visited baby June in the orphanage three times. We would sit out in the garden together and watch the dogs playing. I would feed her her bottle and asked this two-month-old angel if she would like me to be her mother. Her response of course was simply to keep drinking!

Before we had adopted Tashania I was working in a school in Kenya that comprised of mainly Indian children. I can still remember amongst the sea of Asian children with olive skin and silky black hair, this one African girl. Her face and eyes were brown, and her hair would be tied in tight bunches of brightly coloured ribbons. Her name was Tashania. Someone told me later that the name meant 'miracle!' To this day and every day in between, that is exactly what Tashania is ...our miracle.

After my three bonding sessions with Tashania, we decided we would take her home for a weekend. The plan was to then take her back to the orphanage for the week and as I had school holidays the following week, she would come and live with us since then. When we arrived to pick her up, she was ready. Complete with accessory kit. She came with food, bottles, clothes, toys, and a comprehensive instruction manual, which included eating and sleeping times. From the minute she was strapped into our car, and we were driving out of the gates of the home, we both knew that we would not be able to take her back on Sunday. We had a busy weekend, looking for a house help to look after her, as we would both be at work on Monday morning. As nothing is too big, we found one and Tashania never went back to the home. She was ours!

That weekend I called you, knowing you had no idea of my plans to adopt and told you that you were a grandmother. After spilling out all the necessary grandmotherly concerns, like how could I possibly afford to have a baby and what about childcare, you, dad, and my brother were absolutely delighted to be welcoming this angel into the family. Two days later you called back and said you and my brother had booked flights to Kenya, a place you had never had any desire to visit. A new addition to the family certainly changed all that!

One month later I received a parcel from Australia. In those days, the postal system was very slow and there was always the chance that your goods would be stolen along the way. When the parcel arrived, there were a bunch of new clothes for Tashania. Then as I looked further into the package, there were two dresses. One was pale pink and the other lemon yellow. These two dresses had been mine when I was a baby. As tears rolled down my face, I knew this was a sign of the ultimate acceptance of the new addition to our family.

As I write this, Tashania is now twenty-four years old. She will never know the impact she has had on the lives of others. She is one of the humblest people you can meet. She has travelled the world. Grown up attending international schools and through all her life experiences has shaped herself into a truly global citizen. Tashania has friends of all different colours, religions, and ages. People simply gravitate towards her energy and when in her presence feels nothing but joy. As her childhood and adolescent years passed there were many events that occurred that neither one of us could have anticipated. Some of them amazing; some we would rather forget. But both ways we have taken this incredible journey together and we are still on the path. There is not a day that has passed since I haven't been eternally grateful for her presence in my life.

Love and wishes

Susan

MARRIED BY A DRUNK

April 1998, Nairobi, Kenya

"Truth is, everyone is going to hurt you. You just gotta find the
ones worth suffering for." Bob Marley

Dear Mum.

During the three-month fostering period for Tashania, we had
our first visit from the Social Worker who would prepare the
home study report that would be presented to the judge and
would therefore determine our eligibility for Tashania to
become legally ours.

Kenya was still a relatively conservative society in those days
and at the time the Social Worker advised us that the only thing
that might hinder the smooth operation of our adoption process
was the fact that we were not legally married.

Tashania was already ours in both our hearts and minds and
there was nothing too big that would get in the way of making
that process legal. A few weeks after the Social Workers visit,

Mr. Kenya booked a weekend away in a luxury tented camp on the shores of Lake Elementaita. About an hour and a half drive outside of Nairobi settled beautifully in the Rift Valley. This flamingo filled lake was one of my favourite places in Kenya.

As the sun set over the lake, the pink glow of flamingos on the water, changed to a bright orange, followed only by silver shadows that then quickly disappeared into complete darkness. That velvet cover of darkness that only an African sky can bring.

After a delicious meal under the stars, I went up to the desert table and helped myself to two enormous portions of pudding. Upon my return to the table, a small black box lay in the middle of my place mat. As I gently lifted the lid, there inside sat a beautiful Tanzanite engagement ring. There was no need for a question, as we both already knew what the answer was.

On the morning of April, the third, 1998, we all awoke early because we had booked the marriage ceremony for 10am at Sheriah House in Nairobi.

After hearing of the new addition to our family, two of my dear friends from school had booked a trip to Kenya. I thought it would be lovely to have them in Kenya to share my day, so we arranged the date to coincide with their visit. After the ceremony we had booked a three-day vacation to some beautiful hotels at the base of Mount Kenya where would we all go and celebrate.

We arrived at Sheriah House just before 10am. Outside we were greeted by Mr. Kenya's mum who had endured the six-hour bus journey on very bad roads to be there with us. Mr. Kenya's younger brother and older sister were also there, along with a dear friend of mine who I worked with.

In those days it was rare to use lifts in Kenyan government buildings, for fear of power failures and consequently being stuck inside an overcrowded lift...or worse! Thus, we proceeded up the many flights of stairs until we reached the correct floor. We knew we were on the right floor because we were greeted by scores of African women, most of who were dressed in elaborate marshmallow style wedding gowns, complete with tiaras and veils. Standing next to most of these women looking somewhat unenthusiastic about the prospect of the entire situation were white men from a variety of European backgrounds.

Circumstances that bring such unions together are relatively common across the continent. The men were either working or visiting on holiday. They would go to a bar or nightclub and the beauty of women frequenting these establishments would overwhelm them. The next thing he knows she is pregnant and insisting that they get married.

For the women, hooking up with a Western man opens her world to a place full of opportunities. There is the opportunity to improve her standard of living, by moving into a posh house in one of Nairobi's up market housing estates. He will facilitate her in getting a passport and more importantly visas to countries she could once only have dreamt of. She could afford to educate the children she already had with African men and most importantly one day she would gain residency and more importantly a passport of a Western country.

It is my belief that these ideologies are now old fashioned. I may be wrong, but I have a new perception that as Africa has developed over the last twenty-five years, its people have realized that there is so much potential within the continent that they can empower themselves without actually leaving.

We pushed our way through the white dresses, towards a sullen looking lady receptionist sitting behind an ancient desk. Files overflowing with papers filled the shelves around her office. An old-fashioned typewriter positioned to the left of her desk. Not a computer in sight. I politely explained to the lady that we had an appointment with the District Commissioner at ten o' clock. She replied that all these people had a meeting with the District Commissioner at ten o'clock and that presently he was in a meeting.

Reversing back through the white dresses, feeling somewhat dismayed and aware of our time frame for getting to the hotel we had booked, we started looking for somewhere to sit. Not only were there no seats, but there was also not even any wall space left to lean against. The only section of wall remaining was outside the bathroom and it was covered with brown fingered streaks. I could only imagine that the bathroom had no toilet paper.

As we proceeded around the corner in search of somewhere to rest, I literally bumped into my dear friend Kylee and her partner Souljah. Kylee who was also Australian had left Kenya months earlier to travel Europe and to my surprise, had returned to Kenya, visited Mr. Kenya at his office and shown up to surprise me.

With tears smudging my mascara, I marched back to the receptionist to ask if the DC had finished his meeting. After another shirty reply I headed back to our spot to wait with my family and friends. After waiting for approximately two and a half hours and my blood almost at boiling point, our party remained standing in a circle in the narrow chair less corridor.

Suddenly a balding African man in his mid-fifties and wearing a dark black pinstripe suit stood on the boundary of our circle somewhat confused as to how he would pass through. Recognizing this man as the DC one of the members of our party proceeded to stand aside in order for him to pass through the crowd. Still confused the man now took four small steps and was now inside our circle. His feet had stopped moving, but as he stood in the center of our group, his body swayed gently from side to side. As the man greeted us all individually in the traditional African manner of a handshake, we were each taken aback by the pungent smell of his breath. All was then clear. Our DC had not in fact been in a meeting. Or if he was that meeting place was the inside of a bar and his clients had been more than a few beers. Our DC was in fact drunk!

Despite his inebriated state, the ceremonies would continue and before too long the first African bride and her party entered his office. After a considerable amount of time and many more African brides later, it was finally our turn. As we walked in, I told the DC that we would like the shortened version of the ceremony, as we had already used up our travelling time to Mt Kenya and we were in a hurry. At that point I was given a marriage certificate to look at and check for any errors. When I saw that they had typed the wrong first name of my father and the wrong last name of my witness, I could have screamed. Instead, I leaned over to my friend and simply told her to sign with the name they had written on the certificate. There was no way I was going back to the receptionist to have it retyped, as I knew through the previous experience with her that such a move would surely be a ticket to the back of the wedding line again.

So, the ceremony began. As the DC swayed slowly from side to side behind his huge oak desk, he explained to Mr. Kenya that in making this decision to marry me now, he was giving up his right of access to other women for the rest of his life. Bigamy was against the law in Kenya. With the stench of alcohol fumes projecting across the desk and into our faces, the DC then proceeded to tell me the same thing regarding men! After the lecture and the exchange of rings, we were married and on our way to Mt Kenya.

Despite the unique experience of the day's marriage ceremony, we were all excited at the thought of three luxurious nights in the Mt Kenya region. There was only one slight problem. At the first hotel that we were to stay in, a British tourist had been robbed and killed whilst walking through the grounds of the hotel, only a week before our arrival.

For those of us living in Kenya in those days, we took such incidents in our stride. We had become so accustomed to them that we no longer let them curtail our daily activities. For my visitors from Australia, who only heard about such things on the news, knowledge of such firsthand incidents could be quite traumatic.

The previous weekend my friends and I had been partying on the dance floor in Carnivore, a bar and restaurant in Nairobi, that also housed a great disco that just happened to be my favourite place to hang out. Remembering that mobile phones were not in Kenya in those days, a phone call came through on the office landline from Mr. Kenya, through to the DJ, who was a friend of mine. The message from my friend leaning over the DJ box and amidst loud music was that Mr. Kenya had been shot and that I should go home immediately.

Racing to the office to call back, the telephone was answered by Mr. Kenya, who clarified the story by saying that someone had in fact been shot at our gate and he thought it best from a safety perspective that we return home.

Telling my DJ friend that Mr. Kenya was in fact fine, we left Carnivore and headed to my apartment in Hurlingham, When we arrived home about two hours after the incident had occurred, the body of a man-an Ethiopian diplomat, who had been leaving our apartments- was still lying covered in the driveway, That night my friends who were obviously so traumatized by the incident took some sleeping pills in the aim of getting some sleep.

Now for my friends this was the second shooting in the space of a week and their whole trip to Kenya was only going to be two weeks in total. We decided that we would try to keep the hotel shooting a secret until after we had left and successfully managed to avoid any newspaper or television publicity around the case! No sedatives were needed that night and my friends slept blissfully unaware, to the sounds of African animals in the jungles around Mount Kenya.

The day after we got back from Mount Kenya, Mr. Kenya's sister had invited us to her place for lunch, before their mum headed back to the village. As my friends sat mastering the art of rolling ugali into small balls, making a thumb print in the center of the ball to then scoop some beef stew into, Mr. Kenya's mother began the conversation.

My new mother-in-law, a fluent English speaker from the Kikuyu tribe of Kenya started to explain to my friends that now that Mr. Kenya was married, his father's tribe, the Luyha from Western Kenya would support him in taking another wife and even a third at a later date. My friends left Kenya the next day to continue with the second part of their trip. Their heads were needless to say throbbing from all the experiences they had had with me in Kenya. We recently met after not seeing each other for sixteen years and re lived those days with fond and life-changing memories.

Lots of love

Susan

ONE OF GREAT STRENGTH AND WISDOM

July 2002-July 2004, Kuantan, Malaysia, Nairobi, Kenya, Doha, Qatar

Meaning of Aaliyah "One of great strength and wisdom."

Dear mum

The adoption of Tashania had been such a wonderful experience for so many people. Tashania's middle name is Hope and we had given her that name as a form of optimism for the future. Tashania had given us seven wonderful years of nothing but happiness, and I felt that we as a family had enough love to share with someone else. Originally when I had first met Mr. Kenya, I had thought that after fulfilling my dream of adopting, we would have a child of our own. For many reasons, adopting a second one felt so natural and just the right thing to do. We had learnt that to be parents didn't mean you had to give birth to the child. Through my life in Kenya, I had learnt that having the baby was the easy part. It was parenting that baby for life that was the challenge. Even now at the age of forty-five my parents are still there for me unconditionally. I recently read that Kenya has the highest percentage of single mothers anywhere in the world. A point I don't feel they should be proud of.

An obstacle to this new idea was the fact that we were no longer living in Kenya. At the time I was working in Malaysia. We used the big summer holiday to travel back to Kenya and start our investigations. We rented an apartment and did what I thought were the necessary moves in setting ourselves up for our second adoption. Mr. Kenya however was not as ready as I was. We were living off one wage in Malaysia, as he was still studying, and he felt the commitment of another child was too big considering our circumstances. We did however manage to do a lot of groundwork that would prove to be useful when the timing was right for both of us.

We visited New Life Home frequently as they had moved within a stone's throw of where our apartment was. We got to know and understand the new Kenyan government regulations and the different systems that had been put in place over the last few years. We met and spoke with social workers, volunteers and nurses who worked for new Life Home and the agency that now headed most of the adoption side of the facility. Little Angels Network.

During this visit I was asked to be the keynote speaker at a function run by Little Angels Network, for past, present, and future adoptive parents. I could offer nothing but positive reflections of my short time with Tashania as her mother and of the incredible impact she had made on the lives of many.

When we lived in Australia, so many people who were trying to adopt overseas children would stop me and ask me many questions about Tashania and our adoption process. For the majority of these people infertility was their reason for not having had a child of their own. Our case was very different. We had never tried to have children. I knew I wanted to be a parent but believed there were various ways of achieving that. For me it was through adoption.

For couples who have struggled with infertility, they often then face the struggles associated with adoption. Many opened their hearts to me and told them of the love and bond they had established with children who had been allocated to them, only to then have the allocation withdrawn. The excessive amounts of paperwork and expense also causes huge pressures on families who at the end of the day really just want to love and care for a child of their own.

New Life Home had become an extremely successful adoption center in Kenya for both Kenyans and ex-patriots. The home and its partners had paved the way to the implementation of child protection laws in Kenya and the streamlining of adoption. They had opened branches in different areas of Kenya and had become a large-scale operation. When we went there in search of our second child, the feeling that this was the right place for us was not felt by me. This is not said to criticize or downplay the incredible work they do. When we were adopting Tashania we needed the security of what New Life had to offer us. This time I needed to look at other orphanages.

My search for the right orphanage ended when we were taken to Missions of Charity, an orphanage run by Mother Theresa's order of nuns. The orphanage was housed deep inside one of Nairobi's many slum areas. On my first visit, we met at a friend's house, removed all our jewellery, left our mobile phones, cameras, and valuables in her house, and set off to the orphanage.

The dirt roads were caked in mud. The chaos of daily life in the ghetto surrounded us. Men pulling mkokotenis laden with goods, women selling fruits and vegetables, shoeless children whose parents could not afford for them to go to school sweeping floors or playing with small handmade wire toys. Preachers reciting verses from the bible on load speakers, goats trying to avoid slaughter by the local butchery and dogs looking for something to eat. As our party navigated the chaos we eventually arrived at the gates of the orphanage. Seated on the only tarmac we have encountered so far, the driveway to the orphanage was a large congregation of women, wrapped in brightly coloured African fabric, small babies attached to their backs, older siblings sitting closely next to their mothers. We literally had to step over the legs of these people to knock on the heavy Iron Gate. I later learnt that the women sat outside every day waiting for either some food from the inside or a donation from someone outside.

The security guard opened the gate, and we were welcomed inside. The contrast between the outside and the inside was incredible. We had just entered a haven of tranquility. To our right was a chapel; to our left was a double story schoolhouse. The inside compound was all tarmacked with trees providing shade from the harsh African sun. As we moved inside, we saw a landscaped Arch housing a large statue of Mother Mary. Walking throughout the compound were the graceful figures of the nuns. Adorned in their traditional white robes, with royal blue band falling softly around the faces of wisdom. We were escorted into the office, where we were introduced to the nun in charge of adoptions. We explained our story and listened to all she had to tell us about the procedure. I knew we had found the right place.

When you adopt a child in Kenya, you do not pay any money for the actual adoption. You pay for the legal fees and additional charges. To pay to take a child from an orphanage is considered buying children. This orphanage functions on incredibly low expenditure. The sister in charge took us on a tour of the establishment. The school that we had passed on our way in educated around 200 children who lived in the surrounding slum area. We walked into a simply decorated room. A large print of Mother Theresa hung in the center of the room. Small round tables and chairs were positioned in one section of the room. Twenty toddlers were either sitting and eating or running around in this space. All these children were available for adoption. They combined the indoor play with an outdoor area that housed a brightly painted playground. We continued along a corridor until we reached another series of connected rooms. One room housed about forty baby cots. Babies lay inside the heavy metal cots, the baby blue paint peeling off many of them. As there were not enough cots to accommodate all the babies, some had to share their cot space. At the far end of the room was a table that had an A-frame with soft baby toys dangling from it. I was told that each baby had about ten minutes a day where they lay under this frame for their stimulation. As we walked back towards the entrance we were taken into the changing room. There was a long table positioned against a wall where ten babies could be changed at a time. In another section was a collection of ten tiny squat toilets, caregivers holding tiny babies over them so as to not have to clean more cloth diapers.

At the rear section of the orphanage was the kitchen area. This area was run by a group of intellectually disabled women. We were greeted by one of the ladies who happily stretched her hand out for me to shake. She seemed pleasant enough however we were told that she was prone to extreme psychotic outbursts. The nuns of the home provided employment, shelter and love to these ladies who would otherwise have had very limited opportunities in Kenya.

As we walked to the third and final section of the orphanage, the sister who was showing us around told us of a child who had been brought into the orphanage the previous day. She was around three years old. When she was brought in, she was extremely disoriented. This innocent soul had been the victim of rape. In those days with the high prevalence of HIV and AIDS in many parts of Africa, there was this twisted belief that spread through many parts of the continent. The belief was that if you were HIV positive and you had intercourse with a baby or young child, you would be cured. This poor innocent girl was one of many African children who were the victim of such a twisted and selfish mentality.

Across the compound we entered the final section of our orphanage tour. This section was by far one of the most confrontational sights I had ever seen. Inside the room were mattresses positioned on the floor of a large room. To my knowledge there were no actual beds. On the mattresses lay the twisted forms of tiny children and babies. Legs and arms were extremely deformed. Many had over or under sized heads. Eyes rolling backwards. Necks unable to support their heads. There were forty children in total. All were victims of attempted termination of a pregnancy that had occurred to late. The tragedy of lack of education for women, combined with poverty produced this group of children who nobody in society wanted except the nuns running this orphanage.

Unlike when we went to the orphanage to choose Tashania, on this particular visit we did not meet our new daughter. After we explained to the sister that we would like a girl who was HIV negative, she told us that there was one girl child who was currently undergoing her HIV testing. If the results of that testing were negative, she would be ours. So, we did not meet her. In fact, I was back at work in Qatar when Mr. Kenya initially met our new child. He took a photo of her and sent it to me. Her name in the orphanage was Joyce. Our name for her was to be Aaliyah. In Swahili it meant one of great strength and wisdom. It is a name that has certainly fitted her perfectly. She is nothing but a ball of strength and wisdom to everyone she touches.

At the time we were adopting Aaliyah, we made our lives unnecessarily complicated, albeit unintentionally. As Mr. Kenya was based in Kenya for the entire period of fostering, we decided to make the most of this opportunity. We had taken out a loan in Qatar and purchased a Toyota Prado that we were shipping from Dubai to Kenya to sell.

We had already flown to Dubai where we went to the gigantic second-hand car souq and purchased the vehicle. After arranging for the relevant freighting to take place we flew back to Qatar leaving the transaction in the hands of the company. Problems arose before the car had even left Dubai. A phone call came through from Dubai telling us that the vehicle we had purchased had in fact been stolen from Japan and was we still interested in freighting it. After a small amount of deliberating, I decided that if the car had made it out of Japan without issue, then this was more than likely a con being played on us by the African dealers in Dubai and that the plan should continue. In my time in Kenya, I had been conned many times. Although I had become sharper to the tricks of con men, this experience was to be the icing on the cake of being conned...or almost being conned.

At the same time, we had decided to purchase a piece of land near the airport in Nairobi. This was the first time we were buying land in Kenya and as we were to discover along the way, this was also a venture that revolved around lies and deceit. The person selling the land to us had been recommended to us through the same lawyer we were using for the adoption of Aaliyah. The story that we were given was that he had been retrenched from his job with Kenya Airways and needed to raise some quick money in order to pay university fees for his son who was studying in Canada. All we would have to do was to pay the duty on the land once we had made the payment. So, we went through all the relevant land searches that need to be done in Kenya. Everything seemed to be in order, so we made the payment. After doing so we were told that a condition of purchase for the original owner was that he needed to pay the duty within three months of purchase. Corruption between land and government was rife in those days. It was common-place for senior government officials to give away land to their tribesmen. People would build houses on this land only to later find them completely demolished due to the fact that they were not the legal owners of the land. Thankfully for us we had not built anything on ours. For us we just learnt that the land we had purchased was not sold to us by the legal owner. Therefore, the transaction was null and void. However, we had lost our money.

Running parallel to this venture was still the adoption of Aaliyah and the selling of the car. In order to sell the car, we firstly had to clear it from the seaport of Mombasa. Corruption was rife and the process extremely tedious. After many trips to Mombasa and huge amounts of unbudgeted bribe we managed to get possession of the vehicle. The difficult part now was to drive the five-hundred-kilometer journey without being robbed of your car. As you now had all the clearance papers inside your vehicle, a person from the port can tell his brother who is along the roadside that this particular vehicle is on its way. If his brother decided to rob you at gunpoint, then you lose your car and all rights to it, as it is completely laden with all relevant ownership documentation inside. Again, we were lucky that we did not meet with any such people along the way.

To sell a car in those days it was commonplace to place an advertisement on a notice board in one of the local shopping malls. People would then respond and come and have a look at the car. This was a highly ineffective way of selling a car and opened the naive seller to a lot of con men and women. So, the con men came and went. Luckily, we had developed the skills of detecting them.

Finally, we had travelled away for the Easter weekend in the car and knew we had a really interested buyer who was coming to see the car upon our return. The lady was a diamond dealer from Mozambique and wanted a nice car to use while she was in Nairobi. She had sent a representative to meet us in a small coffee shop in town to discuss the payment of the car. We entered and sat down. The area was a bit shady and alarm bells were beginning to sound. The buyer arrived and sat down. He reached into his pocket and removed a silver foil packet about half the size of his fist. He slowly unwrapped the packet to reveal small pieces of clear glass inside. He claimed that these crystals were diamonds and that what we needed to do was travel with him across town to a place where we could cash in the diamonds and use that money to pay for the car. I mean seriously! 'What the hell?' If they knew they were coming to pay for a car, why would they have not already cashed in their 'diamonds' and simply come with the cash or met inside a bank to do the transfer?

What they in fact wanted us to do in conjunction with agreeing to their stupidity was to take possessions of these 'diamonds.' As we would then start walking through the streets of Nairobi one of their guys would come and rob us of the gems. We of course were not meant to know that this was one of their guys and we had now lost all of their precious stock. Therefore, we would have to give them full possession of the car as an exchange for their loss. Luckily, we were not so stupid and were not conned by these people. We eventually sold the car legitimately and moved on from that experience. Needless to say, we did not pursue a business of importing cars from Dubai.

The final and most important part of this intricate web we had woven for ourselves was the adoption of Aaliyah. I was still working in Qatar and was travelling to Kenya during every school holiday. Aaliyah was thriving in her new environment.

The first time we had gone to collect her from the home; we were with an Australian friend who was working with us in Qatar and had come to Kenya to share in this monumental event of our lives. On the first day we were told that the home would not release Aaliyah, because she was very sick. They said if she was better, we could come back after a couple of days. Two days later we went back, and she was ready to go. Dressed in the best clothes she had, an oversized red velvet dress with powder blue straw sun hat, stockings and gold hoop earrings that looked as though the dangly part was a map of Africa, she was ready to go.

Aaliyah was tiny. As she had been left abandoned, nobody knew her exact date of birth. They estimated that she was seven months old, and the police had registered her date of birth as the first of April. At seven months she was the tiniest bag of bones. She could not hold her head up and was extremely weak. When we took her home that night, we set about establishing a loving, nurturing routine with her. With both of my children I had always seen that taking a bath or shower with them was a very important part of the bonding process. We had not had nine months to bond during a pregnancy and so we were very conscious of establishing these bonds from day one. After a lovely warm bath, we prepared a bottle and sat down to feed Aaliyah. Aaliyah however, at seven months had never drunk from a bottle and nobody had told us this fact! She didn't even know how to suck. The first night was needless to say a very long one. This poor tiny baby consumed fluids and then started vomiting in the middle of her screams. The following day as I relayed the story to a friend, she explained that perhaps Aaliyah had never used a bottle. In the orphanage they did not have the human resources to sit each baby down individually and cuddle them while they were feeding. In addition, bottles were time consuming to wash and sterilize, so in the orphanage they fed babies from regular drinking cups. Such concepts had never crossed my mind. So, we gave Aaliyah a drink from a cup and low and behold she guzzled away. Following this we simply cut the teat of the bottle to make it larger, so she didn't have to suck for fluid to be released. We gradually reduced the size of the hole and Aaliyah perfected the art of sucking from a bottle.

One of the most amazing things to see in the first couple of months after you have adopted a baby is how they flourish. When we first got Aaliyah, she would flinch at the feeling of touch. She had been touched so rarely in the home, not because of lack of love just because there were so many babies and so few staff. As she got used to the individual love and care that she was receiving from those around her, her cheeks filled out, she gained weight and she even started to smile. It was amazing to see both of my girls blossom in this way when they became ours.

During the fostering period of Aaliyah, I travelled to Kenya around six times. I was very lucky for the Islamic holiday of Eid in Qatar because the way it fell meant holidays were frequent with small bursts of work in between. After our three-month fostering period was complete. I was desperate to have our family reunited in Qatar. It was Easter and I was on holidays again. I headed to Kenya in the hope that those two weeks would enable us to complete our adoption process and have the family back together again. In April, the courts in Kenya close, so our lawyer suggested we file our case under a certificate of urgency. We did not know it at the time, but our choice of lawyer who was not part of the adoption circle in Nairobi at the time was going to make our case extremely complicated. So, we filed the case and were given a date to appear. We showed up and appeared in front of a High Court Judge. Our case was heard, evidence was produced, and we were so pleased when it was announced that our adoption was successful. Aaliyah was now officially ours...or so we thought. We left the court elated and ready so start the next chapter of our life as a family.

Shortly after our court hearing, I needed to fly back to work in Qatar, leaving Mr. Kenya to finish the official paperwork, including Aaliyah's passport in order for them to join us. A visit to the Department of Children's Services to obtain authorization for Aaliyah to have a passport was about to shatter our dreams of being together.

The officer at the Department of Children's Services refused to sign off on Aaliyah's passport. Not only did she deny Aaliyah's passport, but she also claimed that we were in breach of adoption laws. She claimed that we had in fact bribed the high court judge in order to get our adoption approved through the high court and not the family court. Just before our adoption, there had been a huge scandal of a Kenyan pastor who had abducted fourteen Kenyan children and taken them to the United Kingdom where he had sold them as orphans. The scandal made international newspapers and the poor timing led to a huge turn around to our adoption.

The emotional high that we were on from our successful adoption was very quickly shattered. At the time we did not know it was about to get a whole lot worse. As I was based in Qatar and Aaliyah's father was based in Kenya, the Department of Children's Services then decided that we were also in breach of the fostering requirements in Kenya, which stated that a single man could not foster a child. Therefore, the outcome the department concluded with, made the decision that our child who had been in our care for the last three and a half months would be returned to the orphanage. Devastation reigned. I was in Qatar and was hearing this news via a muffled landline telephone conversation. The following morning, I went into my boss's office and asked if I could take emergency leave to head back to Kenya and sort this mess out. There was no way that this baby of ours was being returned to an orphanage. We had fought so hard to get her that we were not giving up now. This was despite the fact that our lawyer.The person responsible for advocating for a better life for this child was telling us to 'just give her back!' For anyone who has adopted a child, you know that the minute that child is in your arms they are yours. Good or bad, they are yours and you are with them until the end.

My boss agreed to leave and yet another flight later, I was back in Nairobi. We quickly discovered that there had in fact been some flaws in our adoption of Aaliyah; however, bribery of the judge was not one of them. We set up house as a family and waited for the social worker to come and do another home study. We personally scoured police stations to get the correct documentation required to state that Aaliyah had been left abandoned and that no biological parent would come back to claim her. While these jobs were incredibly tedious in Kenya, nothing was too big to secure the necessary requirements of our precious daughter. Documentation ready, home study completed, my leave was now coming to an end and yet again I needed to head back to Qatar. I did this with a sense of peace in my heart, knowing that all the necessary procedures had been followed and the only step left was another court case.

The next part of this drama was certainly something that I was not prepared for. As we went to apply for a new court date, we discovered that there was not one judge in the courts of Nairobi who would be willing to hear our case. We had become so famous in the untruths of bribing the high court judge, that there was not another member who was willing to take a risk with us. Devastation turned to heartbreak and despair. 'How would our adoption ever be completed without a judge?' Through the grace of God and after speaking to almost every judge in the High Court of Kenya, a kind-hearted soul agreed to the legitimacy of our case and was willing to hear it.

Another trip back to Nairobi and the adoption of Aaliyah went smoothly. Our child, whom we had in fact adopted twice, was now officially ours. The next step was to get her a passport and get her to Qatar as quickly as possible. This meant another trip back to the Department of Children's Services. Finally, this also went smoothly, and we received all the required documentation of permission to get Aaliyah's travel documents. Thinking that we were finally at a stage to move forward. We were halted with yet another problem. This problem came when we arrived at the immigration department in order to get Aaliyah her passport.

The Kenyan government had decided that they were no longer issuing passports for children who were under the age of seven and who were adopted. What they would issue instead was a certificate of identity that would enable the child to travel. This seemed an acceptable compromise, Tashania had also been issued with such a document when she was a baby and had travelled to Egypt, Australia, The United Kingdom, and other places without any problems. For Aaliyah however the problem was about to become bigger than we could have imagined. When I went to enquire about a visa for Aaliyah to enter Qatar, I was given one final blow, when they told me that the State of Qatar did not accept travel documents as a form of identification in order to enter the country. I came to discover that Qatar was one of the only countries in the world who would not accept this. So here we were resident in Qatar, where we lived and worked, yet our child would not be permitted to enter unless she had a valid passport. At the same time, the country of her birth would not issue her with a passport. I spent hours in various immigration departments in Qatar trying to get them to see reason, however they were completely uncompromising. The law was the law.

Meanwhile in Kenya Aaliyah's father's residency visa for Qatar was about to expire as he had been out of the country for six months. He desperately needed to get back but could not leave without the baby.

His ticket was booked, and he simply had to leave, as the repercussions of getting a new residency visa in Qatar was not an easy one. On the morning of the day before he was due to fly out, he made yet another trip to the infamous immigration building in Nairobi. He had basically been left with two options. He would need to persuade the immigration officials to issue Aaliyah with a passport for her to leave Kenya, or he would have to leave without her. By the grace of God and the touch of a miracle, he managed to successfully obtain a passport for Aaliyah. He was told to return the following morning to collect it. This was the day he was due to travel.

He awoke early and went back to the immigration department. With his heart deeply entrenched inside his mouth, he was given the incredible news that Aaliyah's passport was ready for collection. He called the house and told the housemaid to pack her things. He collected the passport, rushed home, and collected the baby and her things and made his way to the airport. There was only one last hurdle to overcome before our family was reunited...

As events had been so rushed, Aaliyah did not have an entry visa for Qatar. In some cases, this is not a big problem, however in the case of a Kenyan baby arriving into Qatar, she needed to have been issued with a visa in advance. There was no time for this and the risk we were taking here still had some possible consequences. The first one was that without a valid visa would the airline agree to put the baby onto the plane. The second one was what would we do if immigration in Qatar refused to issue Aaliyah with a visa and she had already left Kenys? The first of these scenarios we did not have to face, as I am not sure how, but the airline agreed for Aaliyah to board the aircraft heading for Dubai. In those days there was no direct flight between Nairobi and Doha, something that actually saved us at the time. Knowing that my family would have connection of flights in Dubai bought me some time the following morning to get myself back to immigration in Doha to apply for an entry visa for Aaliyah. Thus, early the following morning, I was back at the tiny immigration office at the airport, yet again applying for a visit visa for Aaliyah and me to be reunited.

We were almost at the end of the academic year and as a family we had already decided to travel to Malaysia and then on to Australia to introduce Aaliyah to family and friends there. The fact that Malaysia provides a visa on arrival for Kenyan passport holders is something we as a family have been grateful for on more than one occasion. Our backup plan had Aaliyah not been granted a visit visa for Qatar was that I would take a flight to Dubai, stay in the airport with the baby, as she also did not have a visa to leave the airport in Dubai. Her father would then take a quick turnaround flight from Dubai to Qatar, where he would renew his visa. He would then travel back into Dubai where he and Aaliyah could then connect from the airport to Malaysia directly and I would finish work in Qatar before joining them in Malaysia for the holidays.

Luckily, we did not need to implement this backup plan. When my friend and I witnessed the immigration official stamp Aaliyah's visa into her passport, we knew we were nearly there. He had only given her a two week visit visa; however, that was all we needed for now, so we were very relieved.

Now the task was to convey the good news to Aaliyah's father who was waiting with her inside the very large Dubai airport. He did not have a mobile phone, so the only way to contact him was by using the airport information desk. Once the call went through, I had to have him paged. Call back after ten minutes, hoping they had located him, and he had made it to the central telephone. I was dropping coins into a phone booth in Doha airport, keeping my fingers crossed that I would find them quickly. This was not to be the case. After calling three times and waiting ten-minute intervals between, I was now running late for work. Not that I would be in a position to concentrate. I now had images going through my head from the movie The Terminal, where I thought my child would be raised inside the

Dubai airport. Finally, after I finished work, I managed to get through on the phone. They had been fast asleep inside the airport hotel, which is why they had not heard the calls over the airport intercom system. That night Aaliyah arrived in Doha. It was one of the happiest moments of my life.

Love always

Susan

PHD IN BEING FIRED

Date: My whole professional career...

"There is after all no light without knowing darkness, and
therefore there is no success without first failure." Byran
Pulsifer.

Dear Mum

Someone once told me that there are only three ways out of
employment: retirement, choice and being fired! Over the
course of my career, the latter seems to have been the most
common thread of me having to change employment! Not
necessarily being fired as such, as when you are on the
international school circuit that is quite a subjective ideology in
itself. It could be simply that your contract is not being
renewed, as was the case in all scenarios except one job in
Kenya and my job in Rwanda.

For the case of the Kenyan job, it was my first teaching position.
I was young, inexperienced, and very idealistic. I had been

working in a school that did not in my opinion treat teachers fairly or equally. I was born and raised in Australia, where employment offered a salary scale and equality. Now I was confronted with African teachers being paid less than foreign teachers and African teachers receiving no benefits whereas expatriate teachers got quite significant benefits in many cases. There was a day when the Board of Directors came into the school to conduct an open forum whereby, they asked teachers to be 'open and honest' about their feelings relating to the running of the school. After almost twenty-five years in Africa, I still see the same pattern in such forums where nobody says anything, except for the token ex-patriot who ends up wearing the flack of honesty. In this case I spoke up about the inequality in the salaries and benefits of the teaching staff and claimed the entire situation to be based on racism. As a collective gasp filled the room, everyone except me could already read my fate.

The following day I was called into the HR office and coerced into handing in my resignation. As has been the story of my life with regard to international jobs, I have always been provided with housing by my employer. Thus, when you are asked to leave the job, you are also asked to vacate your house.

As the search for a new job quickly took place, I suddenly found myself homeless and penniless in Kenya. I piled up all my belongings into my small Suzuki Sierra and spent the next month living out of my car. Some nights I would sleep at friends' houses. Others I would sleep in some dirty lodging where the headboard of the room next door would be banging against my wall all night caused by the people who had rented the room by the hour and needed to get on with their business quickly! After around a month of living like this, I found a new job with a much higher salary than the original one and a house, so I was no longer jobless or homeless.

What was to follow however was a very long and tedious court case as the school I had been working for decided to take out a vendetta against me for all the other expatriate teachers who had previously done a runner' on them, in many cases disappearing with car loans, student's files etc. The school was disputing that I owed them money. They were right. I did owe them money for a car loan, however there was also a final settlement that needed to be used to offset the actual amount and this was where the dispute came about.

The school put the matter into the hands of lawyers. Over the next three and a half years, a couple of jobs later and the arrival of Tashania into our family, I have learnt a lot about the Kenyan judicial system. I learnt how to invoke a stay of execution, I learnt where the serious criminals are kept inside the courthouse' and I learnt how long it can take to get a resolution.

Tashania was now almost 18 months old, and I was working in a new school in the suburb that housed the United Nations in Nairobi. I lived about a ten-minute drive away from work. One Friday afternoon I drove home as usual, planning to spend the evening having dinner with my family. As I walked into the house, the housemaid handed me a letter. I read it and then asked her who had been in my house that day. She told me that some men had come, claiming that they were from the electricity company and needed to enter the building to read the meter. In reality these men were what were commonly known in Kenya as 'court thugs.' They had come into my house and tagged everything they could find of value. They had then gone away and prepared a letter for me stating that if I did not pay the required amount of money within a certain time period; they would come into my house and take my possessions.

I was a relatively new mother at this time and as the decade of the 90's drew to a close, Kenya was becoming increasingly more dangerous. Car jacking's were ever more common. One of my friends had been car jacked just before. He was forced to lie down in the back of the car at gunpoint while he was driven around town. They found an ATM and forced him to withdraw the maximum amount possible from his account.

It was extremely unsettling to know that complete strangers could come into my house claiming to be one person and in fact being another. The Kenyan judicial system was also incredibly corrupt and there was just no way I was going to win this case. As a family we decided it was the right time for us to move to Australia.

I have learnt that there is a difference between not having your contract renewed and actually being fired. In Qatar there were about fifty of us who did not have our contracts renewed. This process while not appearing to be particularly ethical at the time, paled into insignificance compared to what was waiting for me just around the corner in Rwanda.

I had finally arrived to what I had posted on Facebook as being my dream job in my dream country. It had been a lifelong dream to visit Rwanda from the time I watched Gorillas in the Mist. I was about sixteen years old at the time. On the trips I had planned to go gorilla trekking when I was living in Kenya, some war or other atrocity would break out and I had never managed. Now it was my chance. The telephone interview with the Head of School began with him telling me that I had worked in Kenya twenty years ago with the current Assistant Head of School and ended with him saying that he would be in Doha on the 12th of January. I knew this job was mine! When I got the letter of appointment, I thought my dreams had come true. I called my dad who agreed to do the financial bailout in Qatar and after some logistical issues were dealt with in Qatar, we were off. Direct flight from Doha to Kigali! We were so excited! Amalia's father was half Rwandan and even though he was not joining us permanently, he had only visited the country of his father's birth once and he agreed to come and settle us in before he headed back to work in Doha. He spoke fluent Kinyarwanda which we quickly learnt was a huge asset in this country where half the population spoke French, and all spoke Kinyarwanda.

Both personally and professionally this was a dream come true for me. I was offered the position of Director of Special Needs and before that I was to be the Acting Head of Primary School. A school with seven hundred children and forty teachers. When I arrived, I knew I only had three months in the position, which had already been assigned to an American lady. I quickly surveyed the current situation and realized that staff morale was at an all-time low. Most teachers were local and despite the fact that their working conditions were considered to be better than that of government schools, there was still a significant lacking self-worth in most of them. At my initial address to the team, I talked about myself and my experiences. I explained that I had come from Qatar, one of the richest countries in the world and that my world of education had previously revolved around employment packages. What you earn, how big your house is, how many air tickets you received each year. When I was leaving Qatar, many people asked me, "How much will you make?" I had taken a massive pay cut to move to Rwanda but what I would make was not in my mind to be measured in financial terms. I stood in front of this team of teachers in Rwanda and told them my response to the question in Qatar was 'what I will make is a difference."

And that is exactly what we did. As a team I led the transformation of a group of downtrodden teachers to a place where they loved coming to work. They felt valued and respected.

They felt safe, listened to, and appreciated. At our end of year lunch (the first such lunch these teachers had ever experienced), I reminded them of what I had told them the day we met. I reminded them that I had committed to make a difference and together as a team that is what we did.

Then I got fired! The Director with whom I had worked very closely called me into his office on the 28th of January. I had recently returned from a trip to Australia where I had left my children and returned to continue with this job. Two weeks after my return and almost a year into my contract I was fired with immediate effect. I was called into his office at 3:45 and told not to return. I walked out of that office without any financial settlement, commitment of repatriation, nothing!

When I arrived home, a letter was delivered to my house accusing me of all kinds of nonsense. On the following Monday, a public holiday for hero's day, I was called in to meet the Director once again. As I walked into his office, I saw that there was a piece of paper, a school stamp, and some pens on the large table in the boardroom. He was trying to cut a deal with me by offering me a small amount of money in exchange for my resignation. I refused his deal. I was not going to be blackmailed into something that was not of my choice. I was committed to this job and this country, leaving was not a matter of choice on my part.

Love Susan

BLOWS TO THE BODY

1999-2019

> "Men are the ones who are given strength by God to protect women. So, if you hurt a woman you are not a man." Bob Marley

Dear Mum.

"If someone treats you like crap, just remember that there is something wrong with them, not you. Normal people don't go around destroying other human beings." Lessonslearnedin-life.com

This is probably the most painful letter I have written to you. I want to tell you what it is like to be abused by a man. I had not been raised in an abusive home, as you know. There were the occasional arguments and some shouting or throwing of objects, but on the scale of things these were pretty insignificant in our eyes.

I am still at a loss for the reasons as to why a man feels the need to belittle a woman to such an extent. One reason that constantly haunts me is that it is actually a reflection of his self-doubt. His insecurities, his childhood wounds. When someone inflicts violence towards an undeserving party who does not have the same level of strength as him, it is simply a reflection of his fear of life. His fear of commitment and responsibility. His fear of being a man and facing the challenges that being a man places on him head on. Instead, a man who abuses a woman is one who is a coward. He would rather dehumanize another person than face the reality of his life's situation.

In my life I have been hit by two different men. The first time was when Tashania was two years old. We had been at your house having dinner. As is very common in Australian culture, when we are sitting with people, we tend to ask a lot of questions about their lives. You and dad had been asking general questions about family and friends, lifestyles and culture in Kenya. In our minds it was a general get to know you conversation. Nothing offensive and nothing that would warrant an argument. This was my first experience of cultural differences to be had in Australia.

As soon as we got in the car, all hell broke loose. Why were such questions being asked? Whose business was any of the answers? As I tried to explain, it was really no big deal. I was very wrong! It was a big deal and as the argument continued, we entered the house. It was late and Tashania was very tired. Voices were raised and tension was very high.

If I remember correctly, as he moved towards me, I pushed him. His reaction to this move was to wrap his arms around my neck and drag me across the room. Tashania who was held in his arms started screaming and I began to sob hysterically. I lay in a broken mess curled up in a ball on the floor while he stood comforting the innocent child and gloating at his manhood.

There are two men who have stood over me gloating at their manhood. Two men who thought that to beat and abuse a woman is a courageous act of being a man. The first one I left. I moved back in with you and did a lot of work on myself in order to restore what I knew was a decent relationship with some flaws. I attended counselling and read a lot of books. The advantage in this situation was that the person in question had the capacity to learn and understand that what he was doing was indeed wrong. That person also did a lot of work on himself. A lot of self-reflection, analysis of family history and upbringing and inherently accepted responsibility for his actions.

The second person who beat and abused me was not like that at all. The second person believed that as a woman I deserved to be beaten. He believed that the beating of a woman is caused solely by the actions of a woman. In this situation there was no self-awareness and no accountability.

When you are in the middle of such a situation, your head tells you that the only safe place to be is out. But an abuser is a very powerful and manipulative individual. An abuser has the lowest self-esteem of anyone on the planet. An abuser thinks so little of themselves that they believe it is acceptable to beat another person in order to raise their own levels of power and control. Then the abuser claims that they are tough, that they are strong and courageous. Actually, in reality the person who is strong and courageous is the victim, not the perpetrator.

I sat on my bed one evening. The baby was asleep in her cot next to me. He came home from work in his usual bad mood. There is something about an abuser and their love of being in a bad mood that facilitates the power they receive when they strike a woman. I think I was reading a book, quite innocently, when some stupid question was fired at me. I can't even remember what the question was, but the pattern of events is always the same. He asks a question or makes a stupid unsubstantiated statement, accusing me of doing something that it totally ill-founded. In trying to defend myself against these verbal attacks, I simply set up an open fire scenario. Can you believe that in a situation such as this, I can't even remember what the point of the argument was? In fact, it is like that with all cases of being beaten.

And so, he removes his belt. A belt that I had probably paid for! The sound of that leather hitting bare skin is unmistakable. As the welts started forming on my body, I curled myself up into that all too familiar ball and waited for it to stop. The noise and disturbance woke the baby. I walked over to her. Picked her from her cot and attached her to my breast.

It was my regular before school duty that I absolutely hated. Why did I have to get to work forty-five minutes before the start to stand at a gate and welcome people who were not meant to be there at that hour? Why was the school encouraging behaviour that we did not want? Even though I enjoyed meeting the parents who were dropping their children at school and greeting the children by name, I begrudged the principle behind why I had to stand at that gate so early in the morning. Despite my feelings, I would turn up for that duty punctually as a professional does.

I had strategically positioned my glasses so as to cover the bruise that was hiding below them. I had applied extra foundation and concealer around my eyes that morning to hide the shameful bruise that lay below. Despite my efforts, my good friend noticed immediately. She reported my eye to her line manager, who reported it to the head of school.

Positioned in my usual booth, drinking my morning coffee, I received a phone call from the head of school. He asked where I was and said he was on his way to meet me and that I should order him a milkshake. Sliding into the booth across from me, he said he knew what had happened. He said the school would pay for me to receive counselling and that I needed to report the incident to the Gender Based Violence Department of the Police.

I was driven to the National Police Headquarters, feeling more concerned that I might bump into a parent from school (many of the parents were high ranking police officials), than for my damaged eye. This was another amazing thing about Rwanda. They actually had a Gender Based Violence Department in their police force, and it was a fully functioning department, free of corruption and designed purely to protect the rights of women across the country. A statement was taken, after which I was attended to by a young Rwandan doctor. As he was recording my details and discovered the name of my workplace, he started rolling off the names of all my colleagues he was friends with. I felt so embarrassed that someone who knew all these members of my team was now being given full disclosure of my personal life, however my upbeat disposition quickly made the doctor realize that I still did not see myself as a victim. He started telling me stories of the shift he had worked the night before. Of the child victims of rape that he had surgically repaired, of the pregnant woman whose baby he had had to remove because the damage caused by the perpetrator had been too great for the soul to survive. I believe attitude is everything. My situation was nothing compared to others. I completed all the requirements at the Gender Based Violence

Department in the central African country I lived in and vowed that I would never put myself into a situation where I would come to such a place anywhere in the world again.

The tears that you cry when you are the victim of abuse are different to any other tears. Each tear represents a piece of yourself that is being stolen from you when another person demeans or degrades you. What did I do? Why would you want to do this to me? I am a mother. I have many people who love me. You would not even treat a dog the way you are treating me.

Then there is this eternal search for reason that I look for in situations such as these. Why would any one person behave in such a way towards another? As I have been on that search for reason for many years, I have come to the conclusion that many already knew without undertaking such a journey. Abuse is all about the perpetrator. Abuse has no connection to the victim. The abuser is a person who is wounded. They have so much hatred for themselves that they deny because they are too much of a coward to face those demons. That abuser takes the pain and frustration of simply being themselves out on their victim.

However, in my case, I refuse to be a victim. I refused to let this cycle of abuse define my story. I refused to let this abuse engulf my identity and my sense of self. Instead, I used this as a way to understand that as a person I do not harbor hatred. I do not hold a grudge. I am bigger than that. What another person does or says to me is nothing compared to the positive things I say and do for others. So, I never see myself as a victim of abuse. Rather, I see myself as the receiver of a life lesson that however painful, taught me a lot about myself as a person and a lot about others.

That is not to say that there are some lessons a person does not need to learn from firsthand experience. In fact, when I look back at my life, I think there are many lessons that I would have been happy to learn through the words of others. However, that was not the case. For the case of abuse, it seems the universe had a plan for me that required me to learn it firsthand.

An abuser has one of the most damaged egos imaginable. It goes without saying that an abuser feeds off negative thoughts and energy. They have this innate power to make any situation into something bad, negative, and destructive. One of the things I have found most challenging about human behaviour in this situation is the way that others will feed into the negativity of that ego and believe it trustingly. Without any comprehension that there are two sides to a story.

In my case it was the relatives who fed into the negativity, thus fuelling the ego and acting as an enabler for such behaviour to continue. I don't know if it is cultural, or if my cultural boundaries have become so blurred that I can no longer tell the difference. The abuser would feed his relatives all kinds of manipulative truths that painted me to be some kind of a twisted psychopath. The interesting thing about this from my side is that these people, none of whom had ever met me and some of whom had never even spoken to me on the phone had grown up with this person. Surely, they knew exactly what he was like? Surely, they knew of his abuse and manipulation? They were certainly not at all interested in acting in the role of mediator as is common in many African societies. These people were simply content to sabotage my family and believe the lies and half-truths they were being told by one as pure gospel.

The 3rd of March, 2016 was my last night in Kigali. As ironic as the entire year in Rwanda had been for me, I spent the night in a Bible study class. Four Kenyans, two Rwandans and myself. Analysing the Lord's Prayer. In my 45 years of being raised and educated as a Catholic, I had never taken the time or had the desire to study The Lord's Prayer. Now as we sat there, our eyes consciously engulfing the words from this page of the Bible, we read "Forgive those who trespass against us." As we discussed the text of the prayer through the Bible study companion guide, we learnt that to forgive does not mean to tolerate. To forgive does not mean to accept. To forgive means you are setting yourself free from the sin that has been committed against you. To forgive does not mean to forget. It means that you are retaking your power and control of the situation. To forgive means you are choosing the path of positivity and productiveness. You are choosing not to be a victim. You are choosing to take a lesson from the situation. A lesson that can be used to strengthen yourself and move forward. I am a powerful individual who had to learn some lessons about myself the hard way.

One of the lessons that the history of Rwanda teaches us is that of understanding, reconciliation, and generosity of spirit. In Rwanda I learnt that where there is a capacity for the deepest of evils within a society or individual, there is also this amazing resilience. While we do not condone evil, we do nothing but respect the resilience.

Love Susan

DEBT

March 2015, Nairobi, Kenya

"Our drive to enlarge our net worth turns us away from discovering and deepening our self-worth." Lynne Twist

Dear Mum.

When I first started writing this letter to you, I thought I was going to write and tell you about debt. Actually, that is what I am going to do, however I really want to tell you about what debt taught me.

Debt can engulf you like a snake that slowly wraps itself around your body and squeezes the very life out of you, slowly suffocating you to a point where you are no longer able to breathe. The debt that engulfed me was never something that I had planned. I had been under the false belief that my job was secure and that the loans I had taken out were ones I was in a financial position to repay. Ok this part of the belief was real. When I had taken out the loans, I did have a good job. Obviously, otherwise the bank would not have agreed to lend me the money. The thought of not being able to repay those loans had never even entered my mind.

By the time I was 45 years old I was fully engulfed by debt and had no idea how I was going to free myself from it. The loans that I had taken out based on my salary in Qatar had not been serviced in almost two years due to the fact that there was not even a minimum salary that could get close to the repayments. I had resigned myself to the fact that I would need to file for bankruptcy. I did a lot of reading about it and contacted some professionals in Australia. Only to discover that in order to file for bankruptcy you had to be in Australia. At this stage of my life, I was still trapped in Qatar with no way out. Even a brief visit to Australia from Rwanda for Christmas was not going to help because I then learnt that you had to have remained in Australia for three months in order to file for bankruptcy.

So, I would be standing on duty in the playground in Rwanda and I would receive call after call from the banks in Australia trying to chase me down. One morning it was John Smith from the call center in Adelaide. After explaining the story to him of being trapped in Qatar and now not earning enough money to service the loans from Rwanda I think he needed more help than I did! He ended up asking me if he could call the embassy or help in any other way to get me out of my situation. I felt so sorry for him. This poor guy with his ever so common name calling from Adelaide would certainly not have expected to hear a story such as mine. The other thing was that I had never disputed paying the loans. Of course, I had wanted to honor them. The entire situation seemed beyond my control. I could not call the banks from overseas because their numbers were 1300. I did manage to email the story once, but never received a reply. When I managed to get an overseas number the story that I would explain to the operator at the other end was so difficult for them to comprehend that we would just reach a stalemate. Of course, they only wanted their money back. What I wanted was to declare bankruptcy so we could close this chapter but neither option was going to be possible in the near future.

So, the debt, like an oil slick spreading across an ocean, continued to spread rapidly. In fact, when I lost my job in Qatar the debt increased because dad had to bail me out huge amounts of money in order for me to leave. Then losing my job in Rwanda left me totally penniless, trapped in Africa and with no end in sight for removing the serpent of debt that was strangling me.

We were now living in one room on the outskirts of Nairobi city. Gone were my six-bedroom houses paid for by the company. Gone was the incredible view that I had from my house in Rwanda. I had lost all my physical possessions. Everything I had built up in Qatar was gone. Everything I had taken with me to Rwanda was also gone. I slept on a mattress on the floor. Had no stove or fridge and ate minimum amounts of food from the small IKEA bowls I had carried for Amalia to use. It was quite a culture shock for me. I had gone from a senior managerial position where I would talk to around one hundred people a day to a living situation where on many days, I would speak to no one. Joanne in her wisdom advised me to view the situation of my new life as a form of camping. That actually provided me with some solace. Not that I particularly liked camping, but what I loved was being in Kenya and despite its challenges, that is where I was.

But let me go back to the beginning of this story of the financial crisis. In the past I had had small amounts of credit card debt accumulated from a holiday or simple overspending. These debts were never unmanageable and were never particularly large. More often than not I could completely pay off my credit card when the statement arrived. In those days, I thought I had learnt from those experiences that having a debt deducted from your salary was soul destroying. I had managed to eliminate all those debts, only to accumulate one that was far bigger than I could ever have imagined. The cycle of debt is almost like an addiction. Not that I have ever had an addiction, but I imagine the two scenarios to be similar. No matter how hard you try to remove yourself from the situation that is engulfing your life in a negative and oppressive way, the forces around you keep you trapped inside.

I had always believed that money is simply an energy force. I believed that money was in fact nothing more than a piece of paper the same as that which we write on and some metal that we would use to mould materials. The difference between the paper and metal that becomes money and that which becomes keys or toilet paper is simply the value that we place upon it. In my early days in Kenya, I had taken a particular liking to West African trade beads. The intricate designs of flowers and the colours of these beads were what were used to quantify their value. I wore with pride my necklace of West African trade beads and loved to tell people how in ancient African times these beads were used as currency. Now money was more than just paper and metal. Money was also a sequence of numbers that would rise and fall inside your computer screen or phone.

I think my belief in the energy flow that is money, is something that helped me to stay calm as I was being surrounded by this enormous debt. After all, it is not really about the debt. It is about the complete lack of control that you have over your life and decisions that is created by the debt and lack of cash flow. In my case when I had taken on the debt, I had a good job and excellent cash flow. Then I lost that job. That was followed by a job that was paying me one quarter of the salary my first job had paid, in addition to the fact that I now had to pay tax and bills, which I had not had to do with my first job. Then as if things were not bad enough there, I then lost that job and was put into a position where I had no means to get myself and my baby from Africa to Australia.

So, I started reading, reading about how to free you from debt. I had already resigned myself to the fact that there was no point in stressing about this debt. I could not control its outcome and I could not control the outcome that was destined for me regarding it. I had tried as best I could to come to an amicable solution to the problem but as bankruptcy was not an option, we could only ride with it. In the Western world, to many people debt is just a part of life. We have a debt on our car, house, renovations and more and more a debt that is accumulated in the trap of consumerism. In Africa debt is totally different. Debt is something that you might have obtained through some form of microfinance that you are using to start a small business or that you have borrowed from a friend and need to repay. In Kenya they have what is called chammas. It is a collective savings program where people contribute small amounts of money, and they then use it to take a loan. This is an excellent system of self-support and financial management.

Through my readings and my newly acquired angles of financial education, I learnt many things. One of the most important is to know what you owe! It sounds so simple, however as the debt grew, much deeper and underlying learning also rose to the surface for me.

As I continued to read Rising Strong, I came to this crude awakening that had never consciously hit me in any of my previous falls in the arena of life. That awakening was that I needed to learn how to ask for and accept help. I had always been the helper. I had always been the problem solver. As Tashania tells me 'The thing about you mum is that you are always the one helping everyone else. You are always giving them money, taking them out, providing emotional and spiritual assistance and you never expect anything in return". The wisdom of my daughter astounds me frequently and whenever I tell her so, she will always reply with the line 'I learnt it from the best!' Tears will roll down my cheeks when I read Tashania's messages on my phone, but this one really made me think. Perhaps this debt was thrown at me to teach me something and take me to a higher place.

The thing about me is that when I help someone, I actually forget what I have done. When I was in Kenya recently, I went to visit a dear friend. On the wall of her beautiful house was this enormous 3D television. I had carried that television from Qatar for her a few years before. Her son and daughter had started an extremely successful business using a camera that I had also taken for them from Qatar. I have paid for air tickets for people, and I guess done many more things that others know more about than even I do. At the time that I am doing such things, I believe I do them from a genuine authentic place. The problem that I have now discovered is that it has been rare for me to put myself into a place where I had had the need to be helped by others. I have always been financially secure. Have always known how to tap into various resources be it books, movies, therapists, who can assist me emotionally or spiritually, that I haven't ever really needed to reach out to people and say, 'You know what...I really need your help!'

The first time I really did it was when Amalia was born. I was so physically broken from her delivery that I was not in a position to take care of myself, her, or my other children.

The second time and on a much deeper and personally more confronting level was when I was completely broke. After leaving Rwanda, I was both broke and broken.

Sitting on my mattress in my small, rented room in Nairobi, dear friends in Australia would regularly check up on me. One of them asked if I was OK for money. Of course, I was not but admitting that was more shameful than I could have dealt with at that moment. I replied saying that if I got stuck, I would let her know. Of course, I already was stuck. We had no food or nappies for Amalia. After a couple of days of agonizing over asking for help and more importantly opening myself up to the realization that I actually needed help. I sent the message. Tears were pouring down my face. Thoughts of shame, fear and failure raced through my head. How had I got to this place? Degrading myself so thoroughly? This debt could ruin my friendship forever, but we were so broke that this is what I was reduced to. So, I pressed send and in doing so had opened myself up to what I considered to be one of my most vulnerable points ever. Within seconds the response came...'of course Susan, I will send it tomorrow!' In reality it was as simple as that...ask and you shall receive. From an internal and emotional level, it was far more of a challenge.

Then you and dad bailed me out again. To be honest I don't think I have ever felt so much shame in my life. Not because you had helped me, but because I saw myself as a failure because I could not help myself.

Susan

WHERE IS MY HOME?

January 2015, flying from Adelaide, Australia to Kigali Rwanda via Hong Kong and Addis Ababa

"Every new beginning comes from some other beginnings end."
                                    Seneca

Dear Mum

It is often said that no journey is complete until you have returned home. I don't think I planned for my journey to ever be complete then! It had never even crossed my mind that I would even consider moving home. In fact, I think I had even forgotten where home was. Was my home in Kenya where I have spent more than twenty years going in and out? Was it Qatar or Rwanda or was my home a new country that I was yet to discover? There are countries that I know systems and procedures. Countries where I can drive on the left-hand side of the road without issue. In my entire adult life, I had never considered Australia to be my home. Australia was a foreign place to me. A place that had systems I didn't know or understand. A place where I felt like a foreigner even though I looked like a local. A place where I thought I was a stranger. Yet why had I never stopped to think about the fact that I had not known or had any of those things in any of the countries I have moved to? When I moved to Kenya, I was a fresh-faced twenty-year-old who had never lived away from home, and I managed. When I moved to Malaysia I went as a single parent, had no car, no money and no friends or networks and I made it. When I moved to Qatar on that 50-degree day with a small child and nothing else, the heat almost melted us into the ground, but we made it. When I moved to Rwanda, I found a country where many spoke little or no English. I had a housemaid taking care of my child and security guard that I could not communicate with at all. I was left in the middle of this central African country alone by Amalia's father, but I made it. So why not complete that journey and return home? There is no shame in doing so. In fact, as an international educator, perhaps it is time to take that education to the people of Australia and teach them about these experiences I have had. To teach them that they do in fact live in the lucky country. To teach them that life is all about a matter of perspective. To teach them that there are people who have little or nothing to eat, who have children who cannot go to school but who do not suffer from the many illnesses and ailments that we in the West seem to be consumed by. Perhaps it is time....

Maybe I will see you soon

Susan

CONQUERING FEAR

January to August 2017

"You don't lose if you get knocked down; you lose if you stay down." Muhammad Ali

Dear Mum

Despite all the experiences I have had abroad, moving back to Australia was conquering one of my greatest fears. I was terrified of anything to do with Australia. I could not consciously explain it at the time, but my life had revealed that it was more of a habit for me to keep running than to face the fear of returning home. I had lived with a huge amount of support in terms of house help and facilities and knew I would not have access to any of this upon my return. I was also moving to a town where I did not know anybody and had no family. Luckily, the small town that I moved to in Far North Queensland had a real sense of community that the minute we got there we knew we were a part of something.

Each school holiday in my first year I travelled back to Adelaide to touch base with friends and family and to let my children bond with their cousins and grandparents. The second set of school holidays was encompassing a trip to meet a dear friend of twenty-five years, who I had met in Kenya and who now lived in Canberra. Then on to Melbourne to collect my children, before heading to Adelaide.

The trip was booked for three people and the day before travel Mr. Rwanda decided he was not going to come. As we moved out of our accommodation and I was lending my car to a friend, his decision was one that made very little sense to most of us. So I went on the trip, caught up with people and then returned to my job and life in Far North Queensland with my son who was now coming to live with us.

From the moment we returned his behaviour was edgy and uncooperative. This was not something new and we had somewhat learnt to deal with his 'monthly cycle.' It was peak tourist season in our region and finding somewhere affordable to live was immediately challenging. We moved into the local pub, and this is where the drama began. He refused to help carry the bags in from the car. This upset me as I was tired and had travelled from far away. I needed to get things organised for work the following day and now with no permanent accommodation I needed to sort the belongings and put them into storage.

So, as he continued to upset me, he pulled his all too frequent stunt of removing his phone and making his usual stream of home videos with me in the position of the crazy person and him as the victim of it all. In the past he had used these videos to send to his friends and family as evidence of my insanity and to build his case of perfection towards himself. There was a time where he had even sent a video to one of my work colleagues who then showed it to me, stating that this is a crazy person who would do such a thing to a woman and video her in an extreme state of distress rather than offering her comfort.

This day was different. Over the holidays when he had decided not to travel with me, he had sought immigration advice as to the easiest way for him to remain in Australia. It had been very difficult to save the eight thousand dollars required for his spouse visa and as he had no concept of money, he did not understand this fact at all. In fact, he thought I had the money in my back pocket and was simply refusing to give it to him. Of course, in his mind every 'white person' has a lot of money and if you are white and working then eight thousand dollars was small change. Those of us who do work in Australia naturally know otherwise. This was something that I was learning more and more as I was interacting with people in Australia who gave me their perspective of reality here.

So, the immigration advice that he had received from a source unknown to me was that his easiest way to stay in Australia would be to seek asylum based on HIM being the victim of domestic violence. There really were no limits to the levels he would take to get himself a visa to stay in Australia. And so, we had returned, and the time had arrived for him to start the implementation of his plan.

As I was carrying the very heavy bags up two flights of stairs at the pub, he shamelessly sat watching me do so. This was another of his regulated behaviours, whereby he would put me into a position that I did not want to be in and without shame would view and often video me through the task. After finishing with the bags, I stupidly tried to talk to him and outline that I did not want or need this behaviour from him at this stage. We had nowhere to live and were about to start the new academic term with my son starting his first day of a new school. And so, his crazy making conversation began. Why do I keep looking for rational thought or reasoning from him during these times? Have I ever in the history of knowing him received that? And yet I soldier on, stupidly looking for what I know I will never find from him. Rationality, cooperation, understanding, Empathy! The fault therefore lies in my searching and yet I continue to search.

The continuation of his crazy making conversation, calling me names, abusing my son, abusing me with all sorts of irrational obscenities that were now ingrained in my psyche, as per usual made my tempers rise. And then when he said he was recording me, I simply snapped. I leaned over him in his seating position, my knee planting itself into his groin while I scrambled for the phone to stop it recording. He pushed me away sharply and I retreated. The next morning, I woke up and prepared the children for school. There was a small incident with my daughter not picking something up from the floor and it triggered me to shout at her. This action of mine sent him completely crazy, shouting abuse and waving his phone at me. At which point I grabbed the toxic piece of apparatus and threw it to the ground, smashing the screen.

As a gut reaction I picked up both children and left the house heading to...well I wasn't quite sure where. I ended up in the office of my boss who agreed that my child could stay in class with me for the day, while I sorted myself out. And then the call came. "Susan, there has been a call from the local police station, and they will be coming to meet you at 9am!"

WTF! I composed myself and waited for them to arrive. There were two, a man and a lady. They sat down and explained that they had had a visit at the station from my husband, claiming that he had been assaulted by me. Tears simply rolled down my cheeks as I looked at the police officer in the eye and said, "He will do whatever it takes to get a visa to stay in this country!'

KNOCKOUT! He had done it again! I was down! Well, the referee had counted to nine, so I still had one count to get myself back up!

I went back into class and continued teaching for the rest of the day. In the afternoon I had to go to the police station to sign the paperwork and receive my date and time to appear in court.

Sending love

Susan

INJUSTICE OF JUSTICE

July 2017-October 2017

"The worst form of injustice is pretended justice." Plato

Dear Mum

He walked out of the small, typically designed Far North Queensland hotel and I did not see him again for three months. One of the teachers from school agreed for the children and I to stay in their garage until we found something more permanent. With a roof over our heads, it now meant I could look for childcare arrangements for Amalia and try to sort out this huge mess before I was required to appear in court. On the day he had reported to the police station of the violent attack against his phone, the policewoman, a lovely local lady had asked him if he had ever been violent towards me. His response had been 'not in Australia,' as though violence towards another is differentiated between countries. While this alerted the police to his ways, they were required by law to continue the process of my case as perpetrator and him as victim. One of the differences here was that instead of providing the victim 'him' with the relevant support mechanisms, the police arranged for a social worker to assist me.

I was also sent to the Women's Legal Centre. On the day I arrived I walked into a huge office and found a young lady sitting over a desk in the far corner of the room. She looked up and greeted me by saying hi. She was casually dressed, and I was not sure of her position within the organization. Not removing her hands from typing, she asked me if I was the victim or the perpetrator. When I told her I was the perpetrator, she picked up a file, came over to sit with me and proceeded to tell me everything I was about to lose in my life because of my violent behaviour. Little did she know of the loss that I had already experienced, and I was not about to sit back and let this person who was not willing to even hear my side of the story sit there and think she had the capacity to ruin my life. I walked out of her office totally dismayed at how a system 'my system' was so conditioned to see everything as black or white when nearly everything about life falls into the area of grey.

Walking out of her office, I felt so deflated. My head was saying...this is my country. I had lived in other countries for the last twenty-five years, where I had been subjected to their laws. Now I was back in my own country, I felt surely 'my' system would support me. I was home. I was meant to be supported! Well as time went on and I moved through various systems in Australia, including domestic violence and bankruptcy, I came to understand that the system is not designed to support us. We are taught to buy into the systemic paradigm of systems being created to support us, but what they are actually designed to do is keep us in a state of fear and that is where we are best controlled by them.

I sat on the beach in Port Douglas and breathed deeply. People around me were telling me how crazy this situation was. Most either knew or suspected how violent he was and felt that what I needed to do was to fight this system and prove myself right. As I sat on the beach breathing, I knew inside me what had happened. I knew I did not need to prove my innocence to anyone. I most certainly did not have the money to hire a lawyer and even if I had the money, I did not have the energy. I was completely broken and when we operate from that frequency what usually happens is, we make really poor decisions that the system can hone in on and take further advantage of our brokenness. The few droplets of energy that I had remaining inside my being needed to be utilized really wisely, or I would very soon be at a point of no return.

His narcissistic supply had been running low just before I left on the trip without him. He had thought I would not go, and he would have won a huge supply. He was wrong! I had not let him ruin my plans. He also knew that having Marley living with us would expose who he was to others. This had already happened once when the children had returned to Australia from Qatar. They had told their father of the hell they had been living through under this man and that's what contributed to him not sending them back to Rwanda to live under those conditions.

He went into his usual tactic of upping his anti and then disappearing. So, while I was sitting in Far North Queensland in the garage of a friend's house trying to sort out the insanity of a domestic violence court case, two small children and a full-time job, he was off chasing women, money and narcissistic supply.

My time back in Australia has taught me how fortunate I am to think outside the box. Many fall unconsciously into the beliefs of the system as being normal and designed to help. I on the other hand am so used to systems in Africa, Asia and the Middle East, that I know they are what they are and that is usually a systemically engrained model to control people while keeping them broken and broke.

On the day of the court case, I dressed as though I was heading to court, packed a snack for the kids who would be waiting outside, as I had no childcare and arrived early. As I stood outside the court room a lady came up to ask me a question, thinking that I was a lawyer. Then a lawyer sat next to my social worker and I and casually asked what I was there for. My social worker reprimanded him swiftly. From his side he thought I was 'one of him.' He didn't realize that I was about to be convicted as the perpetrator of domestic violence. Mr. Rwanda was there. We had spoken many times before this date, and he was back in love with all of us. He spoke to the police officers who asked me what my plea decision was going to be. He told them that we had reconciled and that there was no need for us to go into the court room. He stood with his arm around me as he was told by the police officer that as he had filed the order through a police station, there was no way it could be revoked. And so, we were escorted into the courthouse to await our names being called to enter.

I had three choices with regard to the order. I could plead guilty and be put on a five-year good behaviour bond. I could plead not guilty and take the case to a trial with lawyers and money involved, or I could agree to the order being issued without agreeing to its contents and be put on a five-year good behaviour bond. I agreed to the latter and a few days later received an official letter outlining the conditions of my five-year good behaviour bond.

The familiar hot tears dropped down my cheeks, as he stood next to me receiving copious amounts of his depleted narcissistic supply. With barely enough energy to put one foot in front of the other to walk out of the courtroom, I exited slowly. Marley, all of eight years old at the time walked up to me, slid his tiny hand into mine and said, "mummy are they taking you to jail now?"

Energetically paralyzed, Mr. Rwanda took my car keys and decided he was going to drive us home. That day he moved back into my house, into my bed, into my world.

You see what the system does not do, is have the capacity to deal with the grey (and in my opinion most of our lives are grey). As I mentioned earlier, the system deals with the black and the white. I was guilty, he was innocent, case closed, move on with your lives. The reality of that is, that now as the perpetrator who is in fact the victim, is that the real perpetrator is now fuelled with so much more systemic power that he had not had prior to the court case and this ammunition was about to play out as my complete annihilation.

I read through the list of actions I was now forbidden by law to do or say to him. There were a lot! He took the letter from me and read the list. Well now he was to live in narcissistic heaven because he actually had a legal system in a Western country on his side and he knew, unlike in African countries, this system would follow through on their consequences. I was not permitted to raise my voice, so he would insight situations strategically designed to infuriate me. As an example, he would prepare food for Amalia and leave Marley with nothing to eat, or he would leave the house with Amalia while Marley was in the bathroom and Marley would come out to find he was home alone. Terrified he would head over to a kind neighbour. While I tried to plead the insanity of such situations to him, saying these are innocent children, he would ramp up his crazy making conversations to make me shout.

With the children now settled into school and full-time child-care, this gave him plenty of opportunity to entertain his women in my house and in my bed. After I left Far North Queensland, I heard that two had accused him of rape. He would disappear every night, saying he was going to the gym. In my mind, a non-working individual who has children in full time childcare could go to the gym during the day. Why would you go at night? Oh yes! A narcissist would go at night so they can potentially infuriate the person who they have recently had convicted of violence against them and who is on a good behaviour bond for said offence and who can be put into jail if there is a breech in the order...Enough!...Enough!...Enough!

And he got what he wanted. One Saturday afternoon, he walked into the house having disappeared the day before. And argument had been brewing and he knew how to push the final button to extricate the supply he required to keep himself going. As my voice rose, he followed his ever so regular pattern of turning around and walking out on me. And I followed my ever so regular pattern of following him. At the corner was a police car. They were dealing with an incident, and he barged in on them claiming that he was being harassed by me. The police asked us to wait a moment and I stood shivering, with the all too familiar hot tears rolling down my cheeks. The police came over. The children were both in the house alone and not knowing where we were. I knew they would be terri-fied. The police asked if there was a domestic violence order in place. I nodded. They asked who the perpetrator was, and I replied that it was me. My legs literally collapsed from under me. Mr. Rwanda was set free and strode off proudly down the street. I was a sobbing mess and explained to the police that the children were in the house alone. I really needed to get back. They let me go and I found the neighbour tending to their screams from inside the house.

As if things couldn't get any worse, on his sporadic returns he would rile me up and tell me that he would be coming into my work to tell everyone what I was like. I was now working in the Head office of Catholic Education in Cairns, and I absolutely loved the job and the position I was working in. The absolute humiliation of him doing this to me again, in my own country was just too much to bear. He had done it in Rwanda, where he used to come onto the huge campus and pace the buildings looking for me and telling everyone who got in his way, the latest thing I had 'done.' So, I had a meeting with my boss in Cairns and explained what was going on. Not knowing whether it was related or not, my contract was not renewed after probation, and I was about to be unemployed again.

Love Susan

DEATH SAVED OUR LIVES

November 2017

"A great soul serves everyone all the time. A great soul never dies. It brings us together again and again." Maya Angelou

Dear Mum

Redemption equals forgiveness equals atonement equals peace!

The sudden death of my father in November of 2017, although sounding unusual became the catalyst for many great things in my life. I had never watched a person die before and I had never lost someone close to me before.

The stroke that dad suffered in 2009 was what I now know in hindsight the opportunity for him to heal the wounds he had harbored for his whole life. Louise Hay sights the metaphysical reasons behind a stroke as being a lack of flexibility. And that was my dad to a T. He never did anything he didn't want to do; never went anywhere he didn't want to go and led his life in a way that he believed worked best for him. Now I can see that my dad like many others who roam this planet searching for inner peace would hide behind the façade of his business, which don't get me wrong, showcased his creativity and gave him the connection to others that he craved. He was one of those old-fashioned self-harmers who in those days were not labeled as that, like the teenagers today who try to suppress their unexpressed emotions by taking a razor blade to their arms and engraving patterns to represent the pain. He was of the generation of self-harmers who chain smoked from the days their adult hormones kicked in at around the age of fifteen until he died. He habitually rolled his own cigarettes, removing the packet of Tally-Ho papers and delicately combining them with the blend of Bank tobacco, often times with one knee navigating the steering wheel of the car while he juggled the road and the cigarette.

Dad had just returned from a business trip to Perth. You thought he was asleep on the bed, when police showed up at the door asking if you knew his whereabouts. After looking for him on the bed where you thought you had left him sleeping, it was then discovered that he had just driven his car into the front section of our local library around the corner. To this day we don't know how he managed to get his car into that position, and we are always thankful that nobody else got injured. And so, he was taken to hospital where they discovered pneumonia and soon after they discovered that his body was full of cancer. He was unable to walk; however, the experts had said he would come home once he was able to.

I remember so vividly the meeting I was attending in Cairns where I had been working, when I received the call from my brother saying I should come home as he had had another stroke and the probability of him surviving it was nil. That call came on a pay day which meant there was money in my account to pay for a ticket for Marley and myself. Amalia would stay in Cairns with her father. Although I would have preferred to go alone, there was nobody in my house who would agree to take care of Marley for me.

Dad never came out of that coma. We sat there as he gasped his final breath and slipped peacefully away into a place free of pain and embraced with peace. Before he left that mortal realm, we had blasted the tunes of Bob Marley throughout his hospital room. "Stolen from Africa" resonated through the lyrics of Buffalo Soldier. After my dad had died and I began my journey of healing I was to realise the importance of these words alone in piecing together the parts of the puzzle that had been left unexplained in my soul. After we finished dancing to Buffalo Soldier, my all-time favourite Bob Marley song came on. Redemption Song. It is a song that has always resonated with and through me and today was no different. I remembered the bus journey that Amalia and I had taken just a few years before from Kigali to Nairobi. The powerful lyrics of this song had washed over me as we left the winding hills of my precious Rwanda and embarked on the thirty-nine-hour bus journey to Nairobi. Today as Bob Marley sang in that hospital room, I was losing another powerful source of life, what I didn't consciously realize at the time was the gains the children and I were going to achieve as a result of that transition.

Redemption equals forgiveness equals atonement equals peace! This was now the formula I would use to ensure there would be peace in the hearts of myself and my children.

I gave the eulogy at my dad's funeral. I had no script but as a teacher and a storyteller that is exactly what I would embrace in the telling of this story. At the beginning of this eulogy, I asked the guests to each push their thumb into the opposite hand and close it tightly. This pressure represented gratitude.

The gratitude that we all had for having had this man in our lives for as long as we did. At the end of my story, I asked all the guests to look at a photo of my dad and open their tightly clenched fists to release nothing but love and gratitude into the universe.

At the point of my life when dad died, I was classified under the Australian system as a single parent pensioner, who was bankrupt and had a domestic violence order issued against me. I was technically homeless, albeit living under my mum's roof. I continued to sleep in my fetal position until I realized that this breakdown was the catalyst for my breakthrough.

I lay emotionally comatose in a place that many thought had made me beyond repair. Financially I was bankrupt, emotionally I was bankrupt, and spiritually I was bankrupt. All hope had been lost.

Four months after my dad died, I received a call from the oncologist of my auntie. My dad's only sister who had been estranged from the family for many years and in some form of what appeared to be a Hollywood movie had been called by my brother to come to the hospital when dad was about to die and see him. I had not been there when she walked into the hospital room, but I saw her the next day. She was eight years younger than my dad, a person who had loved tennis and socializing and who had never managed to fulfil her longing to have a husband and children of her own. My personal opinion of my auntie was that her life had been so filled with hatred, anger and pain that it had now manifested throughout her body. She had been broken to a shell by the infestation of cancer which had riddled her body. The beautiful, athletic auntie I had known was no more.

The call from the oncologist told me that my auntie had missed a chemo appointment. They had been trying to call her but to no avail. I needed to go over to her house and see what was going on. Along with one of her cousins we went to the house. It was all closed up and we did not get a good feeling. I called the paramedics and waited for their arrival before we went inside the house.

As the male paramedics opened the door, he could smell the interior of the house and turned to me and said, "It doesn't look good." I am not at all good with things like this and as such let him go upstairs, while I waited outside. I had dropped my children at a park nearby as I had not had anyone to leave them with and I did not want them to be exposed to the potential trauma awaiting us inside.

As the paramedic went upstairs, he found my auntie barely alive. He told her I was there, and she asked that I came upstairs. What I saw was shocking. She was lying in a frail, twisted mess on the floor next to her bed. The paramedic quickly grabbed a bedsheet to cover her cold, naked body and as I entered the room, I could see a sense of peace come over her. There were various tablets strewn all over the bedroom floor and we were later to discover that she had been in that position on the floor for around four days. Her frail body had not enabled her to either stand or crawl to a place where she could reach a phone to call for assistance.

Aware that my children were still left unattended at the playground, as the ambulance was on its way, I rushed to collect them and await the transportation for my auntie to be taken to hospital. At least there she would be fully assessed and kept safe and warm. After meeting with the doctor, we were told that soon she would be on her way home, and we started mobilizing actions to have an aged care plan implemented to assist her with independent living.

Six weeks later I received a call from the hospital advising family to come and say their last goodbyes. Shocked we went into the hospital and sat with her, talking in general. Her softly spoken cousin asked her if things had just become too hard. None of us including the doctor had thought she was going to die just yet. She answered as a tear rolled down her cheek affirming that she had given up.

The following morning was one of the first times in my life that I had looked immense fear in the eye. My auntie had agreed to be transferred to a hospice. By coincidence I arrived at the hospital at the same time as she was being transferred. Engulfed with fear, the paramedic assured her she was in good hands and that she should try to relax. Her frail body and face remained tense. I sat with her in the hospice for the next two days. I talked to her about forgiveness and miracles. Apart from me there had only been two other visitors and a small bunch of beautiful pink flowers.

As I sat at the end of her hospice bed, I pondered many aspects of my life. I had come to understand that we draw into our energetic fields all the people, situations, and events that we require for our own healing. My auntie had set herself up very comfortably financially. However, what was the point of having all those things if you did not have your health to be able to enjoy them? My opinion of her life is that she was always disconnected from the truth of her existence. Perhaps as I was sitting here, what I was drawing in from this was an under-standing of what the truth of my existence was. There were many 'things' that my auntie had as she lay there in that hospice bed. She had more than I did, especially if we were using finance as a measurement of those things.

The last image I had of her remains very clear. Her frail body lying under a brightly coloured bed cover as I looked down the length of her bed, me sitting at the end. The next morning, I received a call saying that she had passed away at 1am that morning. I felt relief. She needed to be free of the pain her mortal existence had offered her, she, like all of us had a right to be in peace and the only way I felt she was going to achieve that was in another realm.

Staring death head on through the eyes of my auntie I learned what it meant to have abundance. My auntie had been told by her doctors that the liver cancer she had was treatable. Personally, I do not believe she died of cancer. I believe she died of a broken heart. You see at the time of dad's death; she had seen the love that had been manifested throughout our family. She had met Marley and Amalia along with my brothers' children for the first time despite them all living in Adelaide. She had been reconnected with Tashania and Aaliyah and she saw all the missed opportunities she had lost as a result of her ways. Redemption was not to be hers in this lifetime. But it was going to be mine...and now I was going to seize it fully!

Love Susan

Two of my childhood dreams achieved. To braid my hair and travel to Africa. Here I am standing on Crescent Island. The Island is in the middle of Lake Naivasha. A lake filled with hippos.

So many people told me this should be the cover of my book. Mt Kenya and me!

In my first year in Kenya I was asked to be bridesmaid in a wedding. Skin coloured stockings in those days in Kenya were black!

The centre of love on our planet. You can see it and feel it in the energy of this place. Both trips to India were brief, but provided me with so much essential healing.

The political unrest in Kenya at the end of the 90's led me to the decision of returning to Australia. Little did I know life would be harder for me back in Adelaide and I left again after two years, believing I would never return.

Marley and I at the Ice Bar in Qatar. In Qatar anything is possible. This was an incredible experience with friends, hot chocolate and ice.

No matter how things ended for us in Qatar, we will always love the place. Marley and Amalia still refer to themselves as Qatari and we had to go back to heal the trauma of our departure. While many thought we were crazy, it was one of the most important things we did during our year of deliberate intention. Seeing friends and familiar places settled our hearts and set the foundation for the building of In2EdAfrica.

*When I asked Amalia "What do you want to be now?"
she replied with "Everything I already am but add
fashion design." At 6 she created her first collection with
some fabrics I had bought 30 years prior in Kenya.*

We met on her first day at Brookhouse school in Nairobi.
She became Tashania's godmother and my partner many
years later in all things In2EdAfrica.

Christmas 2019. Our third trip to Kenya that year. I was financially bankrupt but knew I was the wealthiest person around. We had promised to take Amalia's three brothers on a plane and to the ocean. A first for them! A life changing trip.

My second trip to India. My friend was travelling there
for life saving cancer treatment. She thought she was
going to die. I told her "I'm coming!" I was financially
bankrupt and needed permission to leave Australia. I
was on an extreme budget and thought the plane would
crash. But we did it and we are all alive to tell the tale.

I have always been fascinated with Masai culture. Travelling on safari in 2019 with Amalia's brothers and showing them the beauty and wonder of Kenya was a true gift.

Aaliyah with Amalia's first cousin Muthoni. They had an instant conection.

*Amalia's family and the team who put together the
building of our second school in Korogocho. All related
to Amalia's maternal grandmother who once ran a
school on this land.*

*The In2EdAfrica dance troop was born during the
school closures of 2020 due to the pandemic. Schools
being closed left children already vulnerable at great
risk. The creation of the dance troop gave children a
place to be and an opportunity to craft skills they would
never have developed had schools been open.*

Aaliyah shining her light on the world by activating her purpose.

Amalia was only 6 months old when her three siblings left. When we were reunited they didn't know each other. We worked hard to create a culture of kindness, which led to so many wonderful things.

The simplicity of our building is compensated by the innovation and quality of our programs. These backpacks are made from 100% recycled single use plastic bags. They have an embedded solar panel that connects to a stand to give children light to do their homework by.

In January of 2020 a group who had come to Kenya with me, along with our team on the ground stood in our finished school in Korogocho. Amalia's brothers, uncle, cousins and friends of us all, were ready to begin the new chapter in our lives.

Since watching Gorillas in the mist when I was 16, I had always wanted to go and see them. The dream finally came true in 2019 when my stepson and I did the trip together. Standing in the middle of Africa with these incredible creatures was the most exquisite vulnerability I had ever experienced.

The nuns who gave us the gift of Aaliyah. It was always very important for me that my girls knew where they came from and we would return often. This photo was taken on New Years Eve of 2019. We visited with our guests from Australia. Over the years we have taken all our guests to Aaliyah's orphanage and it has changed them forever.

Back together, living life on a trip to Melbourne to visit Tashania

The first time all four of us had been in Qatar together since I put them on a plane back to Australia in 2014. A place we still call home and that we love with all our hearts.

Lake Nakuru 2019...healed and on purpose!

Morani and Me!

PART TWO

MY YEAR OF DELIBERATE INTENTION

REWRITING THE SCRIPT

And this brings us to the part of the story where I met the spider. I was broken. I had been living in hell for longer than I cared to think, and it was time for me to join the conquest of the spider. It was time to pull myself up and let those frail legs of mine regain their strength to carry me forward on the rest of my journey. I had never been a victim and like the spider I met in the shower, I was going to make it to the top.

From my fetal position at the bottom of the shower, came the breakthrough. Many would call it a breakdown. Society and its view of us would call it a breakdown. Where we are not energetically or physically in a position to function in a 'normal' way. Don't get me wrong, there were many things I could still do in a 'normal' way, even when I was in the middle of my breakdown, I could still go to the shops, make breakfast for the kids, take them to school and kindergarten. I was also really good at feeding my unconscious psyche with its addiction to pain and suffering, mainly through my inability to disconnect from Mr. Rwanda. Despite the fact that he was living thousands of kilometers away, he still managed to suck my energy and life-force. To combat this, what I did during the first part of my breakthrough was sleep. I literally slept for three months. I had moved back in with my mum who while herself was in a state of immense loss and grieving was able to cushion my fall and simply let me sleep.

After three months of sleeping, I began my year of deliberate intention. I didn't really know what I wanted as part of the process, but I knew what I wanted out of it. Peace! Piece (as in my mind was in pieces and I needed it to be whole) of Mind, Peace of Body, Peace. And I was willing to do whatever it took to find it and to rewrite the script of my life going forward that held Peace at its core. What I knew was that in order to find peace it would involve beginning a true relationship with my soul. It was through and with this relationship that I would now be in a position to start rewriting the script of my life. I was now going to be the one who consciously decided on the font, style, and content of that script. No longer was I going to be governed by the default mechanisms that we are programmed with from birth. I saw that those defaults had been the catalysts for my annihilation. I was like one of those paper cut-out people at a shooting range people fire at to practice their aim. I was full of open holes and wounds that were festering and crying out to be healed.

As I uncurled myself from the emotional fetal position, I made the conscious decision to path the year ahead as one of deliberate intentions. I would not do anything I did not want to do. I would not be with people who were toxic or had toxic influences on my being, I would not say things that did not need to be said and I would get to know my true self. The self that was the core of who I was and that had been buried beneath a lot of stuff for a very long time. In my year of deliberate intention, I would heal.

When I look back on the first forty-nine years of my life, I understand fully that I was not the conscious architect of it.

The way I led my life and the experiences that I drawn into it were based around the default conditioning and projections that had been placed upon me by virtue of my birth and upbringing. I had not been consulted onto the architectural framework of my identity. There had been no co collaboration as to what school I wanted to go to or what would be best suited to my style of learning. Instead, I was sent into a school building that I hated, every day for most of my life. Like being sent into a torture chamber between 9 and 3, where you switch yourself into survival mode while enduring the slow and painful energetic death of bullies, reinforced failure, conditions of right and wrong and hypocrisy.

I was not invited to be a co-creator of the religious beliefs I was to hold as I was growing up. I was told I was Catholic; I was taught the doctrines of Catholicism and I internalized more hypocrisy and less understanding as I grew up. As is evident from my life experiences I was caged inside an energetic field of preconceived judgments, guilt, blame, shame, putting the needs of others above my own, living in a story that had been written for me by the default conditioning of people, situations and events that believed they had a right to write my story, when in actual fact the story and how it plays out is written and can be written by me. This writing of the script, however, can only be done through the healing of those inner wounds. Of healing the resentments and betrayals, the need to rescue others and put myself at the bottom of the pecking order. I had been on the receiving end of narcissistic abuse and enough was enough. My soul had been violated, raped, brutalized, as had my body. Enough was Enough!

BEGINNERS MIND

There is a famous Zen practice known as Beginner's Mind. To me, this practice is basically the practice of living in the present moment with a bit of a beginner's guide in actually how to do that. When we are working with the beginner's mind what it means is that we look at every moment with new eyes. When we look at the moment with new eyes it prevents us from rehashing the past, even if the past occurred in the split moment before the one, we are now in. When we use the beginner's mind, we stop ourselves from falling back into old patterns of thinking, behaviour and emotional responses and thus set ourselves up for the mindful practice of present moment.

I have been very good at attaching my thinking to events and memories of the past. Yet when I do this what is created within me is nothing more than pain and suffering. It is like when you feel as though you know the way something is going to turn out because you have been in that situation before and you know how it turned out that time, so you know how it will turn out this time...which is absolutely untrue. I don't know how this situation is going to turn out, I only think I know because I am not looking at the situation from a beginner's mind. The practice of ho'opon'o'pon'oo teaches us to clear our memories from anything negative through a process of internal healing and release of memories. So much easier said than done, but as a work in progress it is certainly not impossible.

In the mind of the beginner there is no past and no future and that is the only possible place to find peace.

CONSCIOUS INTENTION

I began by setting the initial intention of healing. Healing my body, my mind, and my soul. On my way to Adelaide after leaving Cairns I stopped in Melbourne to see Tashania and Aaliyah who were still living there. In a book shop in St Kilda, A Course in Miracles literally fell on my head. I had heard of the book briefly many years prior when Marianne Williamson was interviewed by Oprah and kept referencing the Course. The Course states itself to be a compulsory curriculum. Its purpose is the acquisition of Peace! Perfect, because that was exactly what I was looking for.

When you follow universal laws, you understand that it is the intention with which you give to others and the intention with which you serve others is what will determine the outcome. Thus, in my mind, a year of deliberate intention would determine the outcome leading to the next phase of my life and the lives of those in my care. When you practice yoga many times at the beginning of the practice the teacher will ask the students to set an intention for the class. What I was doing in this case of a year was setting an intention not only for each day, but for each moment within that day.

The first intention was to heal. I was broken physically, emotionally, spiritually, and financially and without looking inside and healing those wounds I would continue to lead my life as a broken person. I would continue to attract brokenness into my life and that was no longer my intention.

The second intention was to develop physical and emotional strength. My body and mind had both taken severe battering's at the hands of various people and I needed to consciously rebuild my emotional and physical strength so I could move forward in my life's journey stronger than ever.

The third intention was to live in the present moment. To enjoy every moment with the people who I loved. Not to take them for granted and think that if I invested very little, I would get lots in return. I understood that intention to invest time and energy into my children would strengthen their resilience, life perspectives and outlook. At the beginning of my year, I could not have ever imagined how powerful the mechanism of healing is on our children. We never heal alone and when we switch from default to conscious living and govern the lives of our children in the same manner miracles manifest in every present moment for everyone in the moment.

So, in making the conscious choice to lead a year of deliberate intention, I got the opportunity to understand the real reason why I do the things I do. What the real reason was for why I think the way I do, and what the real reason was that I behave in the manner I do. And along that journey I learnt a lot about societal brainwashing, environmental conditioning, and choice. I also learnt that it is the energy that I put into my intention that drives my motivation and is then returned back to me, which in turn comes back to those I love. My year of deliberate intention motivated me to be the best version of myself and with that there was never a feeling of lack and only a feeling of abundance. And as I was to discover this is the universal law that is divinely planned for all of us to enjoy.

PUTTING THE PLAN INTO PRACTICE

So now I had this plan in my mind, I had to work out how to put it into practice. First there was the initial matters of income and housing. And as I was pondering these (although it sounds morbid at first) Divine intervention kicked in. Dad dying in November of 2017 became the catalyst for a new script to be written. While it was a devastating shock to my family, my healing has brought me to the conclusion that he planned this as a way to get me out of the terrible situation I had been living in and opened a pathway for the children and I to move into the large family home with mum. So, we were no longer homeless!

And then the thing that I will forever be nothing but grateful for, if you are living in Australia and want to plan a year of deliberate intention...I signed up for the single parent pension! OK that was reducing my previous salary by about eighty per cent, but the abundance that reduction gave me was so huge and could never be measured in financial terms. With a roof over my head and a little bit of cash flow, I was all set to go.

DE-TOX-PART ONE

The curve ball that the universe had thrown at me meant a big part of step one of my healing was to actually de-tox every part of my being. The bankruptcy had accelerated the trajectory of de-toxing my financial status. The flow of money that had been ever present in most of my life as an expatriate had completely dried up. What took more of a toll on my mind during my de-tox process was the de-toxing of my entire identity. I had held onto the insane abuse of my relationship with Mr. Rwanda because I was so vehemently against the idea of being a single parent. I fought tooth and nail to prevent myself from being in that position. I sacrificed by body, mind, and soul to avoid being a single parent, but as I knew on an intellectual level, what we fear we create...and so I became a single parent with a government pension to prove it. Now I was also de-toxing my ideas about myself as a mother, and manager of her own home. I was living under my mother's roof with her expectations and judgments of parenting, schooling and so much more.

Those elements of de-toxing were less debilitating than de-toxing myself from the energetic addiction to pain, suffering and sabotage that had finally reached seismic proportions through my entangled relationship with the narcissist. I read that de-toxing this addiction was often harder than de-toxing from a substance addiction. The relapses can last years or even a lifetime with some people never getting themselves clean. A relapse in this case is not picking up a needle and injecting it back into the vein. A relapse is picking up the phone and calling, opening the channels for rejection, arguments, the all-encompassing energetic head fuck that can keep you battling, returning to the reassurance of the fetal position that in its discomfort provides the only security there is at the time.

I had been a professional, expatriate, partnered, wage earning female, who managed to raise four kids and work full time, travel the world, invest in property in Africa and Australia. Now I was a single parent pensioner, who was bankrupt, completely broke and broken, sleeping back in the bedroom of her childhood in her mother's house, having exposed her children to the abuse and projections of her inner unhealed wounds.

At the beginning of my de-tox, absolutely everything was going wrong, I was constantly arguing with mum, my Centre link payments had not been activated, nobody talked to me (I wonder why) and things were just a mess. I hated being back in Adelaide. My psychologist at the time recommended I look for like-minded people. I thought to myself, my only like-minded people are in Africa and here I am bankrupt and broke, how will I ever get back to them. Thoughts of my dad came rapidly bubbling to the surface. As I was de-toxing my identity, I remembered that he had always spoken so openly of his dislike towards everything I had eventually become. He had not liked educated women, he had not liked teachers, he didn't see why women should be independent. As I continued to explore these perceptions, I understood that they were buried so deeply within my subconscious that I was not even aware they had been there. My dad and I had a pretty reasonable relationship on the surface, and he would have done anything for me. As I went through this process of self-actualization through the death of my dad, I began to understand, that the way I had been treated by Mr. Rwanda was a repeat of how I interpreted I had been treated by my dad. Dad had been a workaholic. I would lie in bed as a young child waiting for him to come home and say goodnight...he never did. With Mr. Rwanda I would never know if or when he would come home from one of his nightly prowls. Dad was driven by money (which is very common for people of his generation). Mr. Rwanda still puts his quest for money ahead of any human in his life. Dad battled his internal demons and struggles with the addictions of smoking and drinking to deflect his awareness from himself and his children. Mr. Rwanda was exactly the same. This process formed the foundation of a huge awakening for me. Mr. Rwanda was in my life to awaken the wounds I had embedded in my being from my past. He came to awaken the patterns so I could step up and heal them.

Then one of mum's friends offered to give me an energy healing. I had never done any of this mumbo jumbo kind of stuff before, however as a shift out of my default, I was open to anything and off I went. As I lay on her table and she put her hands over me, not touching my body, I could feel this beautiful warmth fill my body. Colours started shooting down my arms, purple, orange, green and blue. Lying face down on a massage table she had worked on my body and now came to my head. Still not touching me, all I could see was the most beautiful clear light everywhere. Then the face of my dad as clear as clear, telling me I had always been enough and smiling at me. To this day I cannot explain what happened, but to me it doesn't matter. In that moment, my whole world shifted. I was now protected by angels who would have my back and protect my soul. The next day my Centrelink was activated with a back payment and steady flow of money. Within a year of this healing, I had built two schools and a library in Kenya and Rwanda. It was like a gateway opened, all the blocked energy had been cleared and what was to replace it was a flow of abundance, gratitude, and miracles.

DE-TOX-PART TWO

De-toxing my self-imposed narrative about abuse changed the way I see the world

When I moved back to Australia, I found the mainstream narrative very difficult to integrate into my understanding of the world. In the classroom I encountered children with all sorts of labels placed upon them. People had all kinds of physical health related labels, mental health related labels, labels for absolutely everything. Then people tended to create their narrative around their labels. The attachment to labels meant they were not in a position to heal from the cause the labels were reinforcing within their narrative. The labels were always fear based labels and all required the outpouring of large amounts of money to 'experts' who would 'fix' them. Remove the label and the person could move forward with their life. What I observed however was that more often than not, people became so fixated with the labels that they became addicted to getting more. It was like the labels became a part of the identity of the person. A child with ADHD is labelled with ADHD and therefore does not fit in with the school system because they can't sit still. Is that the child, or is that the school? Surely if a child cannot sit still, it is because the content is boring or not relevant. It is the system that is broken, not the child, but we rarely label the system, we label the people, and the people then define their narrative around the label.

I consciously knew I owed it to myself and to my children to change my self-imposed narrative about what abuse is and how my narrative around abuse was guiding me and my children through this lifetime. This de-tox involved surfacing the laws of quantum healing/physics and the laws of language and literacy as energetic fields. Fields that have the power to create our lived experiences.

As humans we are the only living species to whom the means through which we create our reality are through our words. Words are used to sculpt the way we shape and form our realities, how we analyze and how we respond to the world around us. The words depression, anxiety, cancer are words I had had very limited encounters within my life abroad yet when I got back to Australia, they were such an ingrained part of so many people's narrative. We have become so dependent on words we speak and hear that we have forgotten that peace is found within the silence between the words. We have stopped listening because listening taps us into the source of ourselves and we are so scared to go there, so we maintain our addiction to words and give them the power to shape our reality. In my culture we use words to sculpt the way we form and shape our realities. We use words to analyze and respond to the world and how we perceive it. Those who understand that our reality is found in the absence of words are, I believe the ones who attach to the silence and therein lies the place of peace many are searching for through words.

Our words and thoughts feed into our narrative and keep us stuck as the main character in the story of the narrative we have created in our mind and play out in our world. Then when we share our narrative with others who feed into it, we strengthen the narrative. With my domestic violence if I had maintained the narrative and language of victim and got others to buy into that narrative, I would never have built the schools that I have in Kenya, I would never have home-schooled my children and given them the opportunity to write their own scripts. Instead, I would have stayed inside my narrative and continued its cycle. For the work we do in Africa I stay as far as possible away from words like empower, charity, poor, poverty etc. because the frequency of energetic exchange that occurs through the use of these words implies that people are 'other' than me.

I was beginning to understand that our vocabulary and the words we use hold experiences that we possess and process as our narrative. Words hold a frequency that connects to our thoughts that penetrate our emotions and extend through our lived experience. If I was going to hold onto the words of abuse, violence, scarcity, poverty, then that is the experience I was going to maintain as part of my future narrative along with that of my children. I therefore had to learn how to speak differently to myself about the abuse through a frequency of speaking differently to others about it. This was going to be the only way I could rewrite the script of abuse and move forward on my quest for peace. As we bring the use and application of words to our consciousness, we learn that we create our own reality, because every word we use creates a punch. I was learning that the power of my words had the capacity to keep the physical punches alive in my reality long after I was not being punched. Our words can keep punching and knocking us down or our words can invoke the healing and ultimate discovery of a world of peace. We then learn what words we can and cannot use. For me I needed to change the narrative of the words abuse, betrayal, guilt, shame, honesty and so many more.

I was beginning to grasp the fact of the lower the vocabulary we use the higher our limitations. They take us nowhere and keep us trapped. The low vocabulary keeps us searching for reason, they are connected to an intellectualized rationalization of our purpose, which is never where our purpose is found. This is not the vocabulary of healing. It is not the vocabulary of peace or of purpose. Higher frequency vocabulary takes us to a level beyond words. It takes us to the cellular level of our soul where the nature of the divine works from a sphere of timelessness that holds the laws of the universe at its core. It is here and only here where we find the laws of creation, attraction, cause and effect and the core of our being...Purpose.

Through the process of de-toxing my self-imposed narrative about abuse, I was actually able to ease myself out of the pain and suffering I associated with that abuse. I developed a conscious understanding of the ways I phrase my words and how they are attached to the collective. I understand that every word we say has consequences to ourselves, the people around us and to the collective humanity. Our words carry the energy within them that either halts our growth and development or sets our creativity in motion. My words had the power to keep or to change my narrative. During my year of deliberate intention, it was all about change.

As my healing evolved, so the frequency of my vibration began to shift. People started to notice me. They wanted to have conversations with me and at the same time there were those who found this shift too much of a threat for their journey and I blessed them as they went on their way.

There is a language beyond that of words, and the narrative and freshly orchestrated view I was now discovering about myself, and the world was exciting. This new narrative was more addictive than the addiction to pain and suffering I had previously embodied. This new language was the language of the soul. The language that is found in the silence, not only of meditation but the silence we create within ourselves that connects us to our true source. I became a co-creator of my narrative with the source that is found in the silence in-between words. The language of the soul embodies light and a potency that can be scary and hard to embrace. The language of the soul is a love-based energy, free of fear and full of purpose. Inside the language of the soul is where we find grace and mercy. It is here we find the truth of unconditional love. The language of the soul gives us the strength to be courageous and to stand in our light and create both the inner and outer transformation that the new script requires for the font and style to flow poetically in line with its true purpose.

It was around this time that A Course in Miracles literally fell off a bookshelf and landed next to me.

ACIM teaches that the purpose of relationships has two dimensions. We then hold within us the choice of how we are going to frame that relationship. If we choose from the place of the ego, then the purpose of a relationship is to fail. The relationship will embody us with guilt, shame, and betrayal. The relationship will always leave us as the victim because we are never responsible for anything that happens to us.

In the Course the special hate relationship places us as the victim. He has abused me. He had it in for me. He never wanted to see me succeed. I have been victimized and therefore I am the victim of somebody else's abuse. In the special hate relationship, I do not have to look within, because I am not responsible for what has happened to me. All I need to do is keep looking at him, because my answers lie totally in the other person and the actions that person has inflicted upon me. What the ego does to me when I choose the special hate relationship is to keep drawing me to people and situations that will act as my enablers to remain the victim.

Mr. Rwanda was not responsible for me not feeling good about myself. I knew that just because his body had the power to hurt and abuse my body, but he did not have the power to affect my mind. The only one who has power over my mind is me. I am the one who is wholly responsible for the love and peace that resides inside of me. I do not experience that love and peace because I am the one who has thrown that away.

As I worked on healing my inner wounds so the light of those projections onto others started to dim. I worked hard on developing my understanding of the fact that no matter what another person had done to abuse my body, there was only one person who could abuse my mind and that was me. Once I interpreted the special hate relationship as one that actually served my mind in its awakening then I was also able to shift from blaming the other towards taking responsibility for the fact that this experience was one that I needed. I needed it in order to awaken my wounds so that I could heal them. As I brought those wounds to the surface and sat with them through the pain and destruction they had caused in and to my mind, I was able to heal them. My projections of a lack of self-worth, the abuse of self, the inability to own my value, betrayal, dishonesty, control, ownership and all the other crap I had unconsciously held within my field of infinite energy, so the truth of who I was began shining. And the harder I worked on removing the stains of a dark and tainted past, the brighter the light of who I truly was started to redefine who I saw when I looked into the mirror of myself.

In rewriting my narrative around abuse there were some things I had to let go of. One of them was my need to be right. If I had not let that go, then my mind would still be trapped in the concept of my being abused. If I needed to be right, then I was buying into the narrative of the ego. By shifting this paradigm to one of being responsible for the experience and the fact that I had drawn it in, I shifted to the realm of oneness, peace, and unconditional love and this was not for another person. This became the oneness, peace, and unconditional love for myself.

This was by no means a pain free exercise, however what I also knew was that remaining in the narrative of a victim of abuse, I was choosing to remain in the narrative of being treated unfairly. And if I perceive that, then I am still working on the path of needing to be right. That takes me back into the service of only the ego and not my true self. I fully embraced that I had no control over the fact that my body had been physically hurt by another, but I understood that I could control my narrative around how I was going to move forward with that. And I chose to move forward from a place of unconditional love, no bitterness, no betrayal, no remorse, only unconditional love.

YOGA

A couple of months into both my bankruptcy and my year of deliberate intention, I rediscovered yoga. I had practiced yoga twenty years ago when living in Malaysia and had who I though at the time to be the wisest old Chinese teacher around. Now the universe knew it was once again time for me to reconnect with yoga and so I started practicing.

Naturally, yoga is full of spiritual practices and the one that hit me first and seemed to have been written for me in the phase of my life was the law of detachment. The Vedic tradition of Yoga teaches that the path to happiness and freedom is found in simply (or not so simply as the case may be) letting go! In letting go, it does not mean we give everything we own away, but it does mean we choose to relinquish our attachment to outcomes.

When I had initially considered the idea of filing for bankruptcy I was absolutely shot down in flames. In my new social and cultural environment Bankruptcy was something that was so shameful and would ruin your entire life forever. If you had filed for bankruptcy, it was believed you would never 'own' your own home or 'have' anything ever again. At the time I had thought 'well who says I have to own a house in Australia. I could own a house anywhere in the world if I really wanted to... and who actually said I wanted to own a house anyway!'

The practice of yoga is the practice of evening one's mind. So, as the student releases their attachment, it is replaced with new knowledge and spiritual awareness.

Through yoga philosophy we understand that attachment is based primarily on fear and insecurity. When we forget our true self, we are easily corrupted into believing that we need something outside of ourselves to make us happy.

I had become immersed into a consumer world that was completely unfamiliar to me when I returned to Australia. Although I had lived in countries that had significant amounts of wealth, the consumerism, marketing, and advertising were never on the scale that they are in Australia. In Australia everything is connected to some kind of selling and marketing. Even the morning news on the radio is presented with an advertisement selling some product presented as if it is the news.

My children even started telling me that if I bought them a particular toy, they would feel better. My response was stay feeling bad because you are not getting any more junk. So, I was now immersed into a society that had been indoctrinated to believe that if they had this much money, they would be happy, or if they lost this amount of weight, they would be happy, or if they had this house, car, partner etc. they would be happy. And yet there were so many people around who had these things and were still miserable. Suicide rates were at an all-time high and it was not necessarily poor people who were killing themselves. So often I encountered examples of people who 'had' everything. The house, car, children in private schools etc. and yet they chose to end their lives leaving all those things they had worked so hard for and kill themselves.

I told my psychologist that I was switching my addiction to suffering onto an addiction to yoga. She raised one eyebrow and said that sounded like a pretty good switch. Every day for an hour I would attend a yoga class. I would unroll my mat and lie on the wooden floor of the yoga studio. There my spine was long, and I was fully connected to the groundedness of space. Every part of my body was connected to the earth, centered and long and strong and connected. And from there we would breathe. Something that sounds so simple yet is actually something that very few of us do particularly well. I began to understand that most people don't breathe deeply. They do shallow breathing as though they are gasping for life. Hmmm...and many of them are gasping for life. Whenever my children get hurt, upset, or injured the first thing they know how to do is breathe. Breathe deeply into yourself, your injury, your pain. For it is through that breath that you have the ability to bring in the universal forces and light and breathe out the universal forces of darkness. And boy does that work!

I came to believe that the positions of yoga were metaphors for my life and that if I practiced them at yoga then they would flow over into every part of what I did. And they did not come naturally or easily. I am not particularly flexible physically so everything about yoga for me was and is a work in progress.

I stood as a warrior, breathing in and out. I am a warrior! Strong, courageous, brave. I went from the weak physical position I had been started in, to being able to hold a plank for a few seconds. I am a plank! Strong, determined, solid. I raised my body into the position of the cobra. I am a cobra! Focused, ambitious, free.

Yoga is something that I really believe saved me in so many ways. It has given me some wonderful friends and an outlook on life that embraces unity and peace at its core. Yoga is not about being the best at any of the postures. Yoga is about detaching from the outcome and letting the life flow of the universe take you where you need to go.

DETACHMENT

In the depths of detachment, we find the wisdom of uncertainty. But oh no! In our world we are meant to be certain about everything. Being uncertain is almost unheard of and has created us all into control freaks who are in turn suffering from anxiety and depression and raising children with these same attitudes to life. The certainty offers no wisdom. We over plan our lives to the point where we open our diaries if we want to plan to meet a friend for coffee and where the lives of our children are so planned that there is no room for play, discovery, spontaneity, and the development of wisdom.

From the moment we start working as young adults we are taught to plan for the future. It's like day one of your working career and you are already being indoctrinated to be planning for your retirement. Really! No wonder we have so many people feeling incompetent, not good enough, less than and lacking, suffering from anxiety, depression. Because they are so busy living in the future that they have no time to stop and enjoy the present. So many people do not even know that the future does not exist, the only thing that does is the beauty, peace, love, and joy of the present. The future is merely a fear-based construct designed to keep us on the hamster wheel chasing things that don't exist. Keeping us embroiled in our unconscious state of agony through anxiety or depression. Keeping us believing that heaven is something that we are striving for. Something that happens to us when we die (if we are lucky!). Heaven is simply a thought process that we create for ourselves. How many people have I met since returning to Australia who live a daily existence of hell? Who receive no joy and who give no joy to others? Who are constantly complaining about their kids, spouses, jobs, financial situation, mortgages, who have no conscious understanding of the fact that being half alive and living this future based existence is taking up all their energy and keeping them from living in heaven right now?

The wisdom of uncertainty sets us free from the prisons of our past and gives us the freedom and peace in knowing that right in this moment I am OK and everything in my world is OK. And that is what matters. Uncertainty is our gateway to freedom, yet most people I know fear uncertainty with a passion.

When I filed for bankruptcy almost everything in my world became uncertain. But as time went on and I learnt to maneuver myself, I fell in love with the uncertainty and made it part of my journey towards detachment and therefore peace. The things that became certain were things like the fact that I would 'never' have a credit card (actually a blessing in disguise). I was certain I could 'never' get a bank loan. And who other than the social conditioning I had been raised under and brainwashed into had ever consciously reflected on the necessity of either of these things anyway.

THREE FATIMAS, TWO ABDULLAH'S AND ONE ALI

I received a phone call from a friend who worked with refugees. They ran a program to teach English and they needed a teacher. She asked me if I would be willing to fill in for a teacher who was going away. I felt cushioned by the fact that it was only a month, so I was not selling myself to something I had not intended to do. I also understood that the timing was right for me to get back up onto my professional horse that I had been beaten down from the year before. So, I agreed and with deliberate intention I showed up for my first lesson.

As my first lesson began, I was opened to a world of education that in my twenty-five years as a teacher I had never encountered. I stood at the front of the community hall, pen poised to the whiteboard and thinking that as this was adult education, we could begin with something that incorporated reading, writing, speaking, and listening. That way I would get a feel for where people were at.

As my students walked into the room, I removed my pen from the position at the white board and stood simply looking at them and welcoming them into the room. The stories that were imprinted on the wrinkled faces of my students indicated to me that I was about to learn far more from them than I would ever be able to teach them.

Most of the students in my class were from Afghanistan and all of them had arrived in Australia by boat. Some had been in the country for a few years and others a few months. The majority were over the age of sixty with quite a few around seventy years old. These beautiful old women with their hijabs tightly wrapped around their wrinkled faces would, over the next few weeks provide me with some of the most humbling experiences of my life.

As I began my lesson, I quickly discovered that this was not like any of the other English teaching I had done. For I had never taught people who were illiterate in their mother tongue. These people had grown up in a war zone and had never been given an opportunity to go to school. Therefore, the things that as an educator I took for granted such as holding a pencil, understanding letter formations, and reading albeit it in another language were educational functions all the students I had taught before held apart from the very young.

It was impossible to get to know my students on an intimate level because their spoken English was so poor, we could barely communicate. As the lessons went on however, I was able to incorporate some facets of their lives into my classes and slowly learned how many children they had, where they lived and how long they had lived in Australia.

This was until I met Abdullah. Abdullah was studying at university and needed some help with an assignment. We did the work and then I asked him what his story was. As I had only been back in Australia for a short time, I really didn't know anything about the refugee situation. And so, Abdullah's story began. He had been to school in Afghanistan when the war broke out and his parents knew it was in his best interest to get him out of the country. They employed the services of people smugglers and paid their life savings to save their adult son.

Abdullah took a plane to Indonesia where he was housed until the time was right for him to board the illegal boat that would take him across the ocean to Australia. I had seen such journeys on television but had never actually met someone who had embarked on such a life-threatening journey. The boat left Indonesia with the one hundred plus passengers onboard in high spirits. Abdullah told me that spirits remained high for the first seven days, after which things took a dramatic change for the worse.

The boat seemed to be lost. It was nowhere near its destination and food had run out. The wind had swept the flimsy shade covering into the ocean and the passengers were facing both treacherous seas and weather conditions when the boat started taking in water. Baggage was thrown overboard, and the people were left bailing water out of the sinking boat for the next seven days. Exhausted, weather beaten and starving, an Australian military boat came and rescued all on board. Surprisingly, everyone had survived. The group were taken to Christmas Island and were later brought to Australia. When I first met these incredible people, I had only recently returned to Australia myself and I was really struggling. I was in awe of their courage, their capacity to see so many silver linings and their unwavering gratitude for everything they had now (which was in fact very little) and gratitude for everything they had been through.

WHAT IS BANKRUPTCY ANYWAY?

When I filed for bankruptcy, I did so deliberately! Before I was put into the position of not being able to meet my financial obligations, I don't think I had ever missed a loan payment. So, I would not consider myself to be financially irresponsible. When I first came to be in a position where I could not service my loans (because I was stuck under country arrest in Qatar and my bank accounts had been frozen), I had thought that the only way to solve this problem was to declare myself bankrupt. I contacted financial advisors in Australia and very quickly learned that in order to file for bankruptcy one needed to be in Australia. More than a year into my unpaid debts I had returned to Australia briefly on holiday and with the intention of filing for bankruptcy and was only then to discover that you actually needed to be a resident of Australia which meant having lived inside the country for three months prior to filing.

Now almost two and a half years into my unserved loans I was back in Australia, and I had been inside for three months, so I was in a position to file.

Prior to this I had spoken to many people about my desire to file and there was not one who wasn't horrified at the thought of filing. You see what I was to discover through this experience was the predetermined culturally imposed shame associated with being bankrupt in my Australian society. Over time I learned that an inadequacy associated with money was deemed more shameful than most other 'social ails' we deem shameful. When you are bankrupt you are perceived as the ultimate failure, and the reason why this is so is because we have created a crazy society that believes our personal worth is measured by our financial worth. After all we now buy into the belief system of two parents 'having' to work to pay the bills and make ends meet. Very few people are conscious enough to see that two parents working is a choice made by those parents. And ask most children of double working parents whether they would rather have the latest gadget or spend time with their parents playing a board game or having a parent giving them undivided attention when they are playing sport, rather than the parent constantly checking work related emails on their phones during the match and I can almost guarantee which one the child will choose. Now this in no means presents that a woman should not work.

So, I filled the application form, declared my debts to the review board and shamefully posted my application to the office in Adelaide. I did not tell anyone I was doing this, but in my head, I knew one hundred percent that I needed to learn this experience. It was therefore with deliberate intention that I made the final decision to file for bankruptcy and not spend the next eighty years chasing my tail and getting nowhere in life in order to save face and supposedly eliminate my feelings of shame.

As I started to rewrite the script, I grew so much more conscious of the fact that we are all here to bring something that has never been brought before. We are not actually here to follow the default settings of culture, religion, family, we are here to leave our individual mark on the world, on our children and on the universe. We are here to shine the truth of who we are and through the light of those beams we empower others to shine their light. That is the essence of healing.

BELLY DANCING AND ARCHETYPES

Missing many things about my expatriate life, I decided I would enrol in Belly Dancing classes. I had done this once before in Qatar with a group of ladies and it was great fun. Belly Dancing embodies the feminine energy that is often lacking in our day to day lives. The Belly Dancing teacher was an exquisite teacher and soul and walking into her studio was like walking into an Egyptian Harem. Beaded curtains that swept aside as one entered. Mirrors, life size Egyptian figures and Egyptian artwork adorned the space. As the sounds of Arabic music swelled throughout the space, the gold metal coins of our belly dancing wraps would flick and swish as our hips flowed to the beat of the music.

In a space of the sacred feminine energy, I met some of the most beautiful women. We talked and sometimes after class went across the road for coffee. As we got to know each other more, one of the ladies who had been receiving some of the snippets of my life suggested I should get my archetypes done. My what? I had not even heard of archetypes, however this was my year of deliberate intention, and I was open to anything, so I booked what for me was to become a life-changing appointment.

The program that I did through the Living Attributes Typology was designed around story informing purpose. Storytelling is the beginning of everything. Story defines our social and spiritual development and when we understand that it is our energetic archetypes that creates the architecture of our story, the power to bring those stories to consciousness unfolds.

I began to understand that it is our story that creates the set of values and beliefs that we wear like clothing and that define how we operate within this world. For example, my stories connected to honesty, self-worth, abuse, family, children etc. shaped the way I react and respond to the events the universe throws at me. Our story gives us definitions of culture, right and wrong, good and bad, but until I worked through the process of archetypes and their connection to story, I had found my story somewhat confusing.

I would often wonder how a girl who had grown up in Adelaide, South Australia in a pretty conventional family, with a younger brother, a swimming pool in the back yard and a private school education could end up in Africa with such a deep connection to the people and lifestyle that I became more at home there than I ever did in Australia.

Before I started working on archetypes, I had been for a past life energy healing. The connection to Africa that came out of the first part of that healing changed my life. Lying on the table with a woman I had never met before and never had a conversation with and being told that I had been the female ruler of an Africa civilization and my subjects had been massacred under my rule, literally rocked me to my core. As tears streamed down my cheeks and the healer said I had been imprisoned and whilst in jail I had built a new group of followers based on my wisdom of the experiences I had learned. And here I was now, back in Adelaide having recently returned from Rwanda where I had relived that exact experience.

As I worked through the process of archetypes the core of my being shifted. My archetypical energies were being brought to my conscious awareness and this meant that they would be tools for me to take forward and strengthen the use of my story.

There were so many new discoveries that I made about myself as I became more familiar with my archetypes. As I grew to know and understand myself on an energetic level and as I started to more consciously use my story, my transformation was accelerated. As I awakened my archetypical energies, the energies in others seemed to awaken also. I started to draw in people, situations and events that were pathing the way for me to achieve my higher purpose. No longer was I getting caught up in the drama feeding frenzy that I had been on for so much of my life. Things became so calm, open, enlightening. My avatars had finally been recognized and were ready to be unveiled to the world.

A huge learning for me when I was working on my archetypes was, that it is the energy centers within our being that we need to correct and transform in order for our light body to shine. As I was working on this process, I was also beginning the building of our second school in Kenya. This school was on a piece of land where I later discovered Amalia's paternal grandmother who she was named after had also run a small school.

I found the correlation between the building of this school and the work I was doing on my archetypes quite cathartic. The typology I was learning was on four levels. The foundation, being the physical realm and three levels built upon it. As I had discovered my whole life prior to this moment, my energetic awareness of my foundations had not been as stable as they could have been and how can we build anything without a strong foundation?

We cleared the ground on the land in Korogocho. It had literally been covered with crap. Broken wood, car tires, glass, old mattresses, chickens walking around in the cramped space. It was a place full of darkness. This area was notorious for being the darkest place in Nairobi. Amalia's uncle had been shot dead at point blank range in his late teens in this area, just a few years prior to our development.

As we cleared the ground, in preparation for laying the concrete foundation for the school, I worked on clearing the energetic crap that lay embedded in the darkness within me. In the physical realm my dominant archetype is Healer. As we cleared the foundational space in Korogocho, I corrected and transformed my light and shadow attributes that were awakening the light of my healer. I was clearing the dark baggage of uncertainty, apathy, indifference, conventional, vanity and relapse to the light energy of transforming, modest, innovative, passion, enthusiasm, and conviction. I was correcting the energies from Cowardice to Courage. As the builders in Kenya worked on clearing the crap from the ground and preparing the concrete that would form the strength of the foundation in an area that had previously been weak, I too did the same in my field of energy.

With the foundation drying in the heat of the Nairobi sun, my foundational core was ready to be built upon. Our building in Korogocho was going to have three levels, each on top of the other, each rising towards the light from the darkness of the ghetto. As I worked on my archetypes, I too was building three levels on top of my foundation. In the emotional realm, my archetype was that of a teacher. The first level of our school would be filled with expressions of hope, prosperity, and love.

When Amalia's uncle had first approached me and offered me the use of this land in Korogocho I had felt very restrained. I had worked hard to get Mr Rwanda and my addiction to him out of my system and now it seemed that I was falling back into old patterns. Patterns that involved his family and that would potentially then involve him. However, as I corrected and transformed that restraint from the darkness to the light of expression, the energetic shifts that took place also shifted. Where there had been so much anger from Mr. Rwanda towards me, I was nothing but calm. Where I had been energetically insecure, I was now confident. Where I had felt and lived the doubts of my abilities, I was now one hundred percent assured that this was my purpose and that nothing and nobody was going to get in my way.

As the ground floor of the building was constructed upon the solid foundation of hope and purpose, Amalia's uncle told me that his mother had run a school on this exact piece of land. Before my first trip to Kenya with the children in May of 2019 I had visited my psychic with them and had been told that Amalia had an angel watching over her wherever she was. As the psychic lady described the angel, I knew it was Amalia's grandmother after whom she is named. I saw the same psychic before I returned to Kenya in September of 2019, and she described the exact structure and texture of the building before we had even started construction. There were angels all around!

As the first floor was being constructed in the ghettos of Kenya, I really started to feel the collective rumblings of an activation of light. In the spiritual realm my dominant archetype is the

Enchantress. This was a big one, because in the spiritual realm what I needed to work on transforming the darkness connected to blame towards the light of forgiveness. And as the nails were being hammered into the raw timber in the ghetto, what I did was remove the nails that had been entrenched into my soul from eternity.

My year of deliberate intention had already ignited the spirit in me and as my soul started to shine its authentic self, I consciously worked on my forgiveness. I was shifting from my default suppressed self, where I had been ignorant of the suppression. Where I had felt powerless to write or be in control of my destiny and where I had numbed myself through the attachment to the material without being aware of how intrusive this darkness was on my purpose. I became more perceptive as I worked on forgiveness in baby steps at first.

And then in Kenya we encountered a hiccup. We were building next to an electricity pole and while my son had pointed this out as a potential obstacle at the beginning of construction, I had replied that our construction manager would have pre-empted this and would have it all under control. And I was wrong! Our construction engineer had for some reason not foreseen this as a potential problem. In hindsight he must have and perhaps this was part of his own awakening of how he sabotages both himself and others. That I will possibly never know. So, construction was completely halted, and I started pouring in more money and more solutions.

I forgave the construction manager. I did not blame him. I knew this project was going to be a success and that I was no longer powerless despite the obstacles he may have been throwing at me. I did not try to fight the problem. I saw it as yet another opportunity. An opportunity to bring me to the next step of where I needed to be. I did not blame our construction engineer, the expert in this field for his ignorance or lack of awareness. I simply sat with the scenario. And the longer I sat in that place of forgiveness, for myself and others, what had perhaps been a problem initially was now becoming an opportunity. Within a short time, the fabulous people from the ghetto came up with a solution and we were ready to finish the construction of that level.

What had been quoted as being a two-week project turned into about ten weeks. Woven into the physical manifestation of the building had been perceived injustices, betrayals, theft, conflict and more. However, I had made so many energetic shifts between laying the foundation and the completion of the project, that there was very little, if anything that came up that I received with anything other than gratitude. This was because I had shifted from a problem focused narrative towards an opportunity focus. I was beginning to understand on a cellular level that it was not the destination I was seeking, it was the instantaneous moment of the constant now, that brought such enormous gifts to myself and the overall development of the project.

So, along the journey of archetypes and building a school in a ghetto in a third world country, I was introduced to my flawed characters. What I had not been aware of was how intimately my flawed characters and I actually knew each other; however, it was a knowledge we had trauma bonded through in my sub conscious. Now I was facing them head on with an introduction into the conscious part of my being.

As this was my year of deliberate intention and not my year of continuous trepidation, I was totally prepared for this introduction. In my physical realm I was introduced to my people pleaser. The energy that is always 'Doing' for others. Whose behaviour is connected to being a do-gooder, a victim, and a rescuer. The people pleaser in me was the field that would make me physically and emotionally drained because I did not have the capacity to say No! At our conscious introduction, I embraced my people pleaser. She was certainly giving me a lot of perspective on my life up until that point. At the same time, she created an understanding in me of the fact that what I now needed to embrace from her was the lesson and motivation of practicing reflection and self-care. At our meeting, I was also awakened to the fact that it was the people pleaser part of me that was blocking my purpose of being that Change Agent, which was my truth.

The second of my four dominant flawed characters that I was to meet on this day went by the name of Drama Queen. While I initially struggled with her dominant characteristics of needing an audience for her drama to be played out in front of, anyone who has read part one of this book would more than likely see that as a crystal-clear part of who I was. The Drama Queen is larger than life. Attention is found even when not consciously seeking it. Well that pretty much summed up my life and so I lovingly embraced my Drama Queen and practiced her lesson and motivation. I would now live an expressive and jubilant life, where the true core of my educator could shine her light on the world.

Risk Taker was my third flawed character. Welcome, welcome, welcome! This one I had no trouble embracing and having a bit of a laugh with. The risk taker is always shifting the benchmark, pushing the boundaries just to see what would be on the other side of them. The risk taker is a disruptor, whose behaviour can be seen as rebellious and who gets easily bored with the norm. I loved my risk taker! She had taken me hitch hiking from Nairobi to Zanzibar, she had encouraged me to get married without telling my parents, like it was no big deal and she had encouraged me to adopt a baby without being married or really having a plan. While I absolutely feared the idea of having a mundane life, I embraced the lesson and motivation of the risk taker and began taking mindful and purposeful actions. And guess what? As I did so the truth of who I am in the spiritual realm was given her opportunity to shine her light. As I became conscious of the role my risk taker had played in my life, I now walked the bridge for my Humanitarian to take her rightful place.

My fourth and final flawed character that I was introduced to on this day was my Attention Seeker. The field that drew attention to me rang true. Again, perhaps not consciously, but as a result of the decisions I had made for myself. Namely positioning the greater part of my adult life as a white skinned person in a sea of dark skin. While there is nothing to do with skin colour per say, in Kenya there were many white privileges adorned to me by virtue of my skin colour. The colonial legacy had been strong through my life in Kenya and while it often worked in my favour, there were also many times when it did not. Either way I would constantly receive attention. As I welcomed my attention seeker into my conscious awareness, I embraced her lesson and motivation and knew that moving forward I would only seek genuine connections. In embracing my four flawed characters lovingly and consciously I felt prepared to move forward in my truth as a Connector, Humanitarian, Educator and Change Agent.

In the ghettos of Nairobi, we were clearing old energy and replacing it with new, fresh, light, optimistic energy. In September of 2019 I sat on the top of the incomplete wooden structure, high above the ghettos, looking out. I sat there with my stepson, the son of Mr. Rwanda and two of Mr. Rwanda's brothers. We had all cleared old energy and replaced it with new, fresh, optimistic energy. We had transformed cruelty into kindness and as we sat there, we no longer saw the ghetto as a place of darkness. The ghetto is a place of hope and where there is hope there is light and for that we hold nothing other than gratitude for every part of the experience.

EMOTIONAL DETACHMENT

When one learns to be mindful, one learns how to be aware of everything that the present moment contains. When we are mindful, we teach ourselves to be consciously aware of how our body, thoughts, emotions, and soul is feeling in any given moment. Through this our perceptions, assumptions and habits become conscious parts of our being rather than remaining in a state of unconscious. When we are mindful, we are basically aware. When we are mindful, we are not looking to push away what is going on within us. We are not looking to devalue it; we are simply looking to be mindful of it. Through this practice we can bring ourselves to a point of emotional detachment.

During my time with the narcissist, I spent the greater part of six years in a state of emotional paralysis. While I had always been quite an emotional person, before he tore out every part of my being, I was pretty much able to control a lot of the emotions. I could scream and shout and release all that needed to be released and then move on pretty quickly. No grudges, no nothing. The moment was done, and life moved forward.

The difference when you are in a state of emotional paralysis is that you have literally had the life force sucked out of you to a point where you often cannot move let alone function. The number of days I could not go to work, or showed up for work and had to leave, the number of nights I would sleep in a fetal position on the kitchen floor while he slept soundly in the bed.

So, as I became more awakened and more conscious of being mindful, I began to understand the processes of emotionally detaching. However, in order to do this, I first had to work through long standing inner wounds associated with guilt, shame, and self-worth. For they are the emotions that are connected to the thought processes that infiltrate our minds and then create the emotional connections that cause us to continue a cycle of self-sabotage.

Emotional detachment is certainly something that I have not found easy and which I believe is something that will be a bit of a lifelong process. To emotionally detach from a situation where a father lets a child down and I am left to clean up the tears is never an easy one. However, the harder it is the more important it is because if we do not get ourselves to a point of emotional detachment then we are constantly controlled in an unhealthy manner and therefore so too are those children we are trying to protect and raise in emotionally healthy ways.

INDIA

Going to India in October of 2018, did not really have anything to do with going on a holiday. India had never really been a dream destination for me in the way Africa was. I had however been to India a few years prior to this trip with a dear friend and it had changed my life. She is British Indian and a Muslim and the two of us went on a short yet life-changing trip, discovering the romanticism of India while also discovering so much about ourselves and each other on the journey.

When my dear friend told me that she would be travelling from her home in Kenya to India for a serious cancer treatment that was not available in her country, I felt so drawn to seeing her there that the pull surprised even me. I was standing in the car park of the center where my children have trampolining lessons, and she was in a major hospital in Kenya receiving her last batch of chemotherapy. Needless to say, she was terrified about what she was to face. The irony of where we were when we were having this conversation was almost as crazy as the words coming out of my mouth over that phone line. "You know what. I heard recently that the Dalai Lama had told a famous Australian celebrity when she told him she had cancer that this cancer was a gift! If fact when she told him she had cancer his response had been congratulations!" Naturally both my friend and the celebrity were left perplexed at this way of looking at something as life threatening as cancer, however I am so pleased to say that in looking at it this way amazing things occurred. Firstly, when you look at cancer as a gift, you are initially breaking out of the preprogrammed model of viewing dis-ease. By looking at cancer from a different perspective and by reprogramming your thought processes and patterns regarding the dis-ease both the patient and their loved ones can come to a place of peace, gratitude and an in depth understanding of what happiness means to them.

I have come to believe that cancer can hit us in many different forms. While most commonly cancer hits us in the form of an uncontrollable division of abnormal cells spreading in different parts of the body. Cancer is also known as a destructive, even evil practice that is difficult to control or remove. This destructive practice can come in many forms, from toxic and broken relationships to divorce, child custody battles etc. When we talk about cancer, we use terms like chemo, remission, disease, battle, survivor etc.

My cancer hit me in the form of a relationship that I drew into my life that was so toxic that it spread poison through every cell in my body almost killing me. My cancer like many others needed intensive treatment to rid me of the contamination that had taken over my life and had the potential for me to lose not only my life but also everything in it that I recognized as important.

My cancer infiltrated every cell in my body in an attempt to poison me. My cancer almost killed me twice. Once in Kenya and once here in Australia.

But you know what...without my strain of cancer my life would not be where it is now. I would not have my beautiful daughter, I would not have many of the people I now have in my life because of my cancer, and I would not be at the place of higher consciousness that I am working towards as a result of the healing I have had to do because of these toxins in my body, mind, and soul.

So, what I feel now for my cancer is eternal gratitude. Without even knowing it, he gave me some of the greatest gifts I have ever received. He pushed me to my limits, and I rose stronger. I believe this to be true for all people who overcome their cancers no matter what form they come to them in. I also believe that I am only in remission. My cancer can return at any time, and I only hope that when it does, I have healed myself enough to understand the thought processes that led to the emotional manifestations that poisoned my body.

I recently read this: "We all get what we tolerate, so when we decide we are no longer going to tolerate it changes occur". Thus, when you know within your soul that you have tolerated enough shit and learned enough lessons, you can make a conscious choice to see things differently, to think differently and to grow. After all, those previous thoughts and behaviour patterns did not serve a healthy body, mind, and soul...

I believe when we take the steps towards doing this, we become not only cancer survivors but cancer thrivers!

So, the journey to India was my equivalent of climbing Mount Kilimanjaro. I had three children who I was ultimately raising as a single mother along with the help of my mum. I was receiving a single parent pension from the government, of which I was eternally grateful, however which was hardly enough money to be travelling around the world on. In addition, I was officially one year into my bankruptcy and when you are bankrupt you have to get permission from the government to leave the country. Australians may associate this with someone like Christopher Skase and expatriates working in Qatar would associate it with the never-ending task of applying for an exit permit when wanting to leave the country.

So, I needed to find someone who could take care of the children, apply to the government for permission to leave Australia and find the money for the airfares. As I wrote an email to my friend telling her that I had quite a lot of obstacles to overcome in order to actually get myself to India, I was awakened to my selfishness. What I had to overcome! What about what she had to overcome? She had just undergone six months of intensive chemotherapy, had a complete bone marrow transfusion and had stem cell replacement and here I was with the audacity to tell her that I had a lot to go through!

The conscious awakening that occurred in this precise moment led me to another understanding of happiness and its cause and effect. While letting go of judgment and competition are sure fire ways to increase happiness, so too is letting go of the programs of self-righteousness and self-absorption. I honestly don't believe in comparing one person's pain to another. I think everyone's situation is unique to them at the time they are experiencing it. However, I do believe strongly in getting ourselves to a point above ourselves where we can see our situation for what it really is, no matter how bad the perception of that problem is at any given time. For me, my situation was all about financial accessibility and potential governmental bureaucracy. Nothing about my situation was life threatening and just simply changing my view from one of deficit to one of abundance meant anything was possible for me in this situation.

I called my bankruptcy trustee and asked about the process of applying to travel. In the conversation I outlined how grateful I was for the experience of being financially bankrupt. How this experience had taught me about what was truly important in life and that going to India to support my friend was one such example. One hundred and fifty dollars later and I was approved to leave Australia for ten days.

India transformed me as a person. I was at the Taj Mahal, the universal center for love and as I placed my hand on one of the gigantic marble pillars, I could feel an energetic force fill my body. It was like every person who had contributed to the building of this magnificent structure, every person who had visited it over the last few hundred years had all left a piece of themselves there energetically to fill me up and prepare me for the next part of my journey.

After the telephone conversation with my friend from the cold car park in Adelaide I felt so drawn to write her a letter...

My dear friend.

How lovely it was to speak with you. I have felt very drawn to write to you and share some of my recent learnings in the hope that they may help you on this journey you are currently facing.

Having removed myself from the most destructive and soul-destroying relationship with Mr. Rwanda, I have spent the last few months on a journey of healing.

On this journey I have learnt that Mr. Rwanda was drawn into my life as a mirror to show me the areas of myself I needed to work on. Mr. Rwanda tells everyone how much he hates me. Through this I have discovered what it truly means to love. I have learnt that God has a predefined plan for all of us, however in order for us to download that plan our heart must be open to unconditional love. So, if we have any elements of things such as fear, anger, betrayal etc, then we have to resolve those matters for our heart to open. Thus, as Mr Rwanda holds so much hatred, his heart can never open, his plan can never download, and he therefore lives a life of chaos.

I now see that Mr Rwanda has been my greatest teacher to date. By treating me the way he did for so long, I have had the great privilege of learning so many lessons that would otherwise not have been a part of my curriculum.

When I was capable of shifting my perception of Mr. Rwanda and what he had done to my life, I transformed my reality by understanding that he was a gift. It was not easy to get to that point, however a couple of things really helped. The first was taking advice to pray for him every day for 30 days. In praying for him I changed chemical imbalances in my brain, which set me free of any attachment to him.

A prayer that worked so well went like this:

Loving and Forgiveness Release

I.........do hereby forgive.........

I release them to bring their highest good and set them free.

I bless them for having been willing to be my teacher

I sever all unhealthy attachments to this person and send them unconditional love and support.

So, the two main reasons I am telling you all this is:

1. I watched a lady recently who was diagnosed with cancer for the second time. She went to see a spiritual practitioner in Tibet and when she told him she had

cancer the first thing he said was congratulations! She was like...what do you mean congratulations! And he then explained to her that cancer was a gift sent to her from God to teach her what she needed to know and to get her to a higher place of self! She is still here and now runs a thriving wellness center for others with cancer where her testimony gives them hope (This is actually an idea I had for that land in Ngong...to start a wellness center where people go to do yoga, massage etc.).

2. Mr Rwanda was my cancer. He infiltrated every cell in my body and tried to poison me. He almost killed me twice. Once, when we were in Kenya, and he physically tried to strangle me and the second time here in Australia where I was on the verge of a complete nervous and emotional breakdown.

But you know what...without Mr. Rwanda my life would not be where it is now. I would not have Amalia; I would not have you and I would not be at the place of higher consciousness that I am at now as a result of the healing I have had to do as a result of his presence. So, what I feel now for Mr. Rwanda is eternal gratitude. Without even knowing it, he gave me some of the greatest gifts I have ever received. He pushed me to my limits, and I rose stronger. And that is the same as you. First your stroke and now this. What it means in spiritual terms is that God has the highest of high plans for you and he has to test you because he knows you are going to get there. So, what I now understand is that life is happening through you and not to you. This cancer is a gift. It is part of God's divine plan for you.

So, here is one of my observations about how I believe you see yourself. I think there are still some blockages in your emotional energy fields because there is this part of you that still thinks you are not worthy of things like love, honor, and abundance (don't worry, we are all like that!).

I have been doing a lot of yoga, meditation, and internal work and one exercise I did was visualizing removing all the band aids I had placed inside me to cover all my internal wounds. As I visually ripped off all the band aids, I was left raw. I had to face things like betrayal, grief, hurt, pain, anger, and I had to make peace with them, so I no longer needed the band aids. By addressing them I found peace.

So, for you. If you actually take this time in India to connect with your inner self, you are at a far greater advantage than me. You will have your blood flushed out and your cells repaired so you can actually be a completely new person when you return to Kenya.

I read this recently "We all get what we tolerate, so when we decide we are no longer going to tolerate it changes occur". And you know what my dear friend...you and I have honestly tolerated a lot of shit! And we are now empowered to make the choice to no longer tolerate it! It is actually life changing.

I was recently listening to this guy. Dr Deepak Chopra is a medical doctor and spiritual practitioner. He is a leader in Mind, body medicine. He knows there is more to healing the body than just taking mainstream medicines. He has written books like Ageless Body, Tireless Mind, the seven spiritual laws of success, Grow Younger, live longer. He believes that while medicine has many of the answers it does not have the technologies to teach them how to change (and this is about changing the mind). He is a practitioner of Ayurvedic medicine and incorporates mainstream medicine with traditional Indian practices.

What is it?

- Ayurveda is an Indian health practice thought to be more than 5000 years old. It consists of a number of disciplines, including aromatherapy, diet, herbal medicine, acupuncture, yoga, massage, meditation and balancing of energies.
- The word "ayurveda" is translated from Sanskrit to mean "the science of life".

He talks a lot about the dis-ease within our body as being a manifestation of our thoughts and energy. In a day we have at least sixty thousand thoughts and the problem is that most of them are the same as the ones we had yesterday. Thus, if we change the way we think and perceive things then we can change what is happening within our body. In this article he was talking about the fact that the body replenishes all its cells about every seven days. So physiologically we are given new fresh cells every week. So, if this is scientifically proven why for example does a cancer stay...because our mind is telling us it is meant to be there! Through your chemo working God is also telling you that your cancer is not meant to be there. But you are being told that you need to learn the lesson of addressing those inner wounds and take yourself to the next level of life.

When my dad died, it was so sudden. I truly believe God planned that for me and that it was Divine intervention. My dad knew (on an unconscious level) that if Amalia and I had stayed with Mr. Rwanda any longer the outcome would have been very different.

About a month ago I was driving to yoga and I got a suicide message from Aaliyah my fourteen-year-old who was living in Melbourne with Mr. Kenya. I was devastated and could not believe it. This little baby who I had taken from Missions of Charity in Huruma. Who had been left abandoned in

Zimmerman and then it was me who had failed her! But divine intervention took place again. We moved her to Adelaide, and she started a new school yesterday. She is warm and loved and has Marley, Amalia, my mum, and I to care for her. I could not even imagine a world without her in it.

So, I think I will finish and get this off to you. Let me end with this...

I CAN CHOOSE TO SEE THIS SITUATION DIFFERENTLY!

You are not a victim of cancer, nor do you even have cancer.

You are the most amazing, resilient, strong woman who is empowered with a tough life lesson sent from God, and specifically designed to take you to the next level of amazing, which is where you are meant to be!

Love and Light Always...Susan

My friend had lived through hell in this lifetime. On the day before I was to leave India, we sat together in her hotel room and wrote thank you notes to all of the doctors, nurses and careers who had treated her. As I penned those notes, she told me the intimate connection she had created with each and every one of them. We wrote of the beauty and joy that she had experienced in every moment as they removed her cells, grew new ones, and replaced her body to a point where she was completely regenerated on a cellular level...and so was I.

My friend left India a week after me and lives the life of a true wise, African healer. She shines her exquisite radiance and truth on everyone she touches and is a complete blessing. She, like me now lives every day in heaven, because we have both made the conscious choice to never live in hell again.

FORGIVENESS...

I have come to believe through the many 'crazy' experiences I have had throughout my life that the only true way to be happy is through forgiveness. Easier said than done in many cases! For me, our world has become so caught up in ego-centered activities, programming, and mindset that we have lost sight of the detrimental impact the ego has on our body, mind, and soul. You see the ego has a powerful role to play in our lives and more often than not we are not even consciously aware of what it is doing. It is our ego that sets a deliberate intention to prove and reinforce to us that we are unworthy, that we deserve to feel pain and to suffer because we are full of sin. It is the ego that reinforces our need to defend ourselves from attack. The law of the ego is that we are separate. Through its separation the ego justifies, controls, blames, shames and in doing so it denies us our right to live a life filled with love and peace. While I understand that there is a place the ego plays in our human existence, if that place is governed through default, instead of consciousness then unless you are a narcissist, there will be a lot of suffering.

Forgiveness is an attitude. It is the sum total of every experience we have collected and stored and the capacity to let that flow outwardly rather than storing it inwardly. I believe forgiveness is a learned behaviour. It is reconditioning the conditioned behaviors that have governed many of our perceptions. Forgiveness is not about saying sorry or accepting the apology of another, forgiveness is the ultimate action of courage.

So, as part of my year of deliberate intention, I set about learning what it actually takes a person to forgive. Almost like a course (that I now believe should be a subject in schools...not as part of religion, as part of humanity and freedom).

From my experience forgiveness is a process of unlearning. It starts by applying a conscious connection to the thought process of forgiveness. This is followed by actions that when practiced repeatedly rewire the patterns of the brain in such a way that forgiveness becomes your default patterning, rather than what had previously been the opposite.

Forgiveness is for you...it is all about you! Nothing about anybody else!

One of the first things I had to do was to develop an attitude for forgiveness. In a famous clip between Oprah and Marianne Williamson, Marianne teaches Oprah that the divine plan for our higher purpose has been written for us from the time of our birth. The thing is that the plan cannot be downloaded onto our screen until our heart is open to unconditional love. And unconditional love is created through forgiveness. Oprah offers resistance, to the thought of forgiving someone who she feels has wronged her, siting that forgiving is way too hard. Marianne asks whether it is easy to hold onto the resentment, bitterness, betrayal, guilt, shame. And therein lies the point! We can't do both and we need to choose which one will serve the greater purpose of living in a state of peace.

While learning the steps of forgiveness is not easy, the long-term reward is nothing other than the creation of an abundance of miracles and who in their right mind would choose anything other than that.

There were three main steps that I applied to my forgiveness process.

Identify

Let Go

Replace

The first event I identified, that had me engulfed in the pits of despair and guilt that was so consciously in my zone was connected to Amalia. At 44 years of age, with two adopted children and one biological, two girls and a boy it may appear that I had everything. I had experienced adoption, I had experienced birth, I had experienced girls and I had the experience of a boy. I had a professional career, an amazing life full of travel, experiences, and laughter. My bills were paid by my employer. It seemed my life was the ultimate experience. So why on earth would I get pregnant? But it was more than that. How could I, a seemingly intelligent, worldly, complete adult bring a child into the world with a man who was so violently abusive. Who had no respect for women and who I knew would not be there to support me or the baby on the journey forward with life.

Just before the start of my year of deliberate intention I was absolutely paralysed by the metaphysical guilt connected to Amalia and her place on earth. I would sob in my sleep, I would sob when I bathed her, I would sob when I was driving her. Put simply the pain of what I believed I had done to Amalia by creating her was so all consuming that it fed into the energetic paralysis of my breakdown.

As I continued to study A Course in Miracles, I became awakened to the millions of forgiveness opportunities that were presented to me. From the person cutting me off on the road, to the people who had inflicted physical pain on my body, mind, and soul, but my first step in the process of forgiveness was to forgive myself. Not only for what I thought I had done to Amalia, but what I thought I had done to all my children, my friends, my exes, everyone who had played a role in my life.

As I identified something I needed to forgive, so more and more forgiveness opportunities came into my life. As I lay on the table having a past life healing, I was presented with a literal lifetime of forgiveness opportunities that it seemed I had brought through from many lifetimes, and I had never forgiven. The residual energies from these lifetimes had built up in my energetic frequency and were literally blocking my purpose with their density. Boy this was going to be a long and painful experience. But it actually wasn't as long or as painful as I had anticipated.

After I identified what I needed to forgive and had chosen to start with the forgiveness of myself for the things I perceived I had done to Amalia and many others, the second step was to let go of all that was keeping me embroiled in the pain and suffering connected to a lack of conscious willingness to forgive.

As a parent it is very difficult to let go of attachment, but I decided that was the first thing I needed to do. It was not letting go of being a guide for Amalia and my children, but it was letting go of the attachment of default ideologies that I had unconsciously adopted and were actually contributing to the pain and suffering. I did this by doing more and more work on myself and my forgiveness. As the year and as time has gone on, I have fully understood that as parents when we stand in our purpose it gives our children permission to do the same. After all it was never me who decided children should go to school at 5. That was a default conditioning I had been fed and I had bought into. It was not me who said education is acquired inside the four walls of a school. Again, that and many other ideologies that are fed to us as parents are default conditioning that are designed to keep us embroiled in our unforgiving, fear-ridden existences which only serve to keep us as existing. Let go! Let go! Let go! We were not here to exist! That idea was killing our soul purpose. We were here to shine our light on others, on humanity and onto the world. And that started with the birth of Amalia.

Amalia is the embodiment of everything that is an angel. She and my other children had the god given ability to be kind in the face of cruelty, to be courageous when surrounded by weakness and to feel a sense of gratitude for every person, situation and event that had occurred in our lives. And this is what they came to teach me.

Let go of attachment

Let go of conditions

We are the warriors

TIME

During my year of deliberate intention, I had to decide to give up the systemically designed structure of time. In our Western society time is given a similar value as money, yet both are intangible objects that actually don't exist apart from through and in the creation of our mind. Our conditioning has taught us that time is a linear construct. Hence our continual desire to seek things outside ourselves. We set goals, seek success, look for love. When we switch our concept of time from horizontal to vertical our life changes in that split second. Through a vertical measure of time we have already achieved our goals, we are successful, and we are and have love. For those things are only found within the present moment and the present moment is only found in vertical time. And therein lies peace.

Living in the present moment: Taking one day at a time and really living in the happiness and joy of that very moment is a life-changing experience. I found that when I stopped looking back, a lot of emotions that were attached to those memories didn't have a chance to attack me. Not looking back and dwelling on the could have, should have, would have's, is transformational in the deliberate intention of peace and happiness. Likewise, not looking into the future, meant there was limited distraction from simply enjoying the present moment. I had always been a pretty time conscious person. I worked to a schedule and knew where I needed to be and when. When I projected my schedule to those around me, I discovered that it prevented them from present moment enjoyment. For example, I was once in Singapore on a transit to Australia. The children and I had an amazing day exploring Singapore zoo and the following day showed up at the airport to catch our flight. Trolley laden and three small kids in tow I wobbled up to the check in desk. Handed over the passports and as the lady looked at the screen, she looked up at me and said, "I'm sorry, your flight left yesterday." My response was quite unexpected for the lady behind the counter, because I simply replied with the fact that we had had such a wonderful day yesterday, that it was obvious the universe had planned for us not to be on that flight. She promptly put us onto the next flight, took our passports back and checked us in!

TRIGGERS

Facing my triggers head on:

I discovered that by avoiding my triggers (which I had done most of my life) I was not in a position to heal them. When we are able to move through the pain pattern caused by the trigger, then we experience healing. When you can do this, you are put into a position of consciously rewriting the ending to that story. I spent a lot of time doing Quantum meditations, where I went deep inside myself and tore off all the bandages that had been strategically positioned since birth.

As I slowly and painfully removed the bandages, I started learning many new and wonderful things about myself. I was starting to join the dots with the wounds and awakening to the fact that if the wound had been healed then there was nothing for the dot to connect to. I was beginning to feel the shift. In the past if someone has insulted me, the first thing I would do was try to defend myself. The worse the insult, the more irritated I would get in trying to put forward my case of defiance against the insult. If the insult was attaching to the wound, then it was creating the dis-ease within my being and acting to disturb my peace. As I healed the wound, the insults would have less and less impact. While the insults have not necessarily stopped, now there is nothing for them to attach to and thus they have nowhere to incubate and grow. I understood that the more wounds there were the more opportunities there were for my triggers to be activated. I knew that if I could be easily offended then I could also be easily manipulated, and these were both dominant traits of who I had always been. These traits however in no way served my quest for peace and they all needed to go.

THE FIRST BIG TEST

"Choose once Again" ACIM

November 2018

"Trials are but lessons that you failed to learn presented once again, so where you made a faulty choice before you now can make a better one, thus escape all the pain that what you chose before has brought to you."

I returned from India at the end of October 2018 just in time for Marley's birthday. By mid-November, the first big test of my healing literally landed on my doorstep. This test came in the form of Mr. Kenya and Mr. Rwanda making independent decisions that they were moving to Adelaide to get back to that all-important job of being a father. Neither knew each other, had ever met and the plan was to keep it that way. I was healing well, triggered less and was much more conscious of my purpose. I decided I could juggle their visits with the children around either of them meeting, even if this was taking place literally on the front doorstep of my mother's house.

Two weeks after Mr. Rwanda arrived in Adelaide, I received a brutal message from his 'partner' or ex-partner, or whatever she was telling me that I had raped him. The next day he moved into a house in the next street from me. I had thought this was a great idea. We could co parent Amalia. Her kindergarten was in-between the two houses and we would integrate the best of both worlds as many had done before us. And guess what...I was wrong!

He believed it was his right as a father to see his young child whenever he wanted to, and he believed it was the responsibility of all around him to facilitate that process. And those around him (being me) facilitated that process from a place of deep-seated emotional guilt, pain, and fear. I had never wanted to be a single parent. And he knew that. But I was one and actually I was doing a pretty reasonable job of it. I was healing myself and through that alone my children had started healing.

Through my healing, I had instilled many boundaries within myself. I was stronger at standing in my truth and he was thrown off balance by my lack of connection, arguing, justifications and defenses of my actions. Those behaviors that had all been normal parts of our relationship were now gone. I helped him look for work and was even happy to drive him to jobs that were far away and too difficult to reach by bus. Before he had secured a house, he would sit next to me in front of my computer while I helped him send-off application after application. As I typed, he would be flicking through photos of the last night's female conquest he had achieved before heading home from some seedy nightclub back to the backpackers where he was staying. That was his business and as long as it did not spill over into that of myself or my children it was up to him how he chose to behave.

Then I got the text message from the woman he had left in Darwin, saying I had raped him and that he is disgusted by me, and I should leave them both alone. Honestly, that was easy enough for me to do. I was well into my healing and if he was continuing to have people in his life who had no respect for his children or his past, that was his to deal with.

The messages continued and, before I knew it, he brought the woman who had been sending me disgusting texts, threatening me and the safety of my child to live in the next street from us. She hated Amalia and hated the relationship he had with her and within minutes of her arrival to Adelaide, everything had changed. This woman was threatened by Amalia and needless to say hated me, so we were back into the familiar pattern of his psychotic behaviour.

I feared that the two of them had come to Adelaide to kidnap Amalia and take her back to Darwin. After all the lies he had fed this woman about me as being the perpetrator of violence against him, this was now her opportunity to save the day.

This was actually quite a terrifying time for all of us. It was summer and we could not roam freely at the local park during the regular entertainment events, for fear that they were hiding somewhere and would kidnap Amalia.

From a Spiritual perspective, I understood that this was the universe testing my healing again. And boy was my healing tested! I spent the first couple of days walking on eggshells in my neighborhood. This taught me the power of my thoughts and their link to my emotional state. I was actually terrified that she would try and take my child from the playground which divided his house and mine. This was of course a thought process which triggered my fearful emotion.

Then I bumped into them in the supermarket. While his face dropped, I proudly shook her hand and introduced myself. She explained that she had been quite a bitch to me, and I agreed (which took her aback). Her messages had been unnecessary, degrading to her and a reflection only of her character.

After a conversation suggesting we have coffee and being declined, I told her that I was so absolutely grateful for the fact that she is in his life. I explained that like his first wife, who I had saved from his torture and abuse, she had now saved me. Through that place of gratitude, I was able to understand my past and whilst visibly shaken from the encounter with the two of them, that sense of gratitude brought me peace for the whole day and into the future.

So, where I had made a faulty choice before, I was now able and equipped to make a better one. I chose self-worth, safety of my children, gratitude, and peace and with those choices so escaped that pain that had been a presence in my past.

CULTIVATING PEACE

"I can choose to see peace in this situation" ACIM

I realized that a big part of the faulty choice I had made over the past forty-eight years of my life was that I had not made the conscious choice to find peace in a situation. I am not sure that I even knew what Peace was. Not the brand of peace that is used for marketing purposes, I am talking about the peace that embodies the physical and spiritual.

In life there are really only two ways we can choose to govern our lives. From a place of fear or from a place of love. There is no in between. All around us however we have nothing but fear inducing indoctrination and propaganda that seeps into our conscious and subconscious mind and teaches us that living in fear is a normal way to be.

With all that going on around us, I believe it is very hard to cultivate a culture of peace within our homes, lives, body, and mind. A peace that permeates through the cells of our being. Having received what I perceived as threatening text messages from the current lover of Mr. Rwanda threatening to kidnap my child, I was encouraged by friends to go into a police station to ascertain what kind of support the system could give me in such a situation.

Upon sharing my story with the lady at the counter I was promptly asked what I feared. I replied telling her I feared he and this woman would take my child and disappear to Darwin. The response from the lady was then...and if he does, he is completely within his rights as he is her father and there is nothing, they can do about it! BAMB! Let's not instil more fear into an already fragile mother who has been threatened. But actually, this is what the system does. It breads fear rather than cultivating peace. Fear makes governments, systems, and industry lots of money. In the Western world we have been taught to fear absolutely everything. We fear, food, death, people, illness, debt, wealth, success, poverty, religion etc. And it is through this fear that we spend billions on medicines to stay alive (but how many times do we hear it is the chemo that actually killed them!). We spend hours checking in for a flight because we fear what 'others' might do on the plane. We keep our kids imprisoned by their devices because we fear letting them play in the streets.

In cultivating peace lives are transformed. Cultivating peace means looking within yourself at triggers, past life histories and e-motions and consciously analyzing what it is that create the fear-based patterns within your being. When you bring them to the surface, no matter how painful that process is, what you are doing is being honest with your authentic self. Through that process you get to know yourself and re program the fear-based patterns that have controlled your life before you were even born. You set yourself free and you discover that there is peace in every situation. Life happens through you and not too you and that our life's purpose is purely to find peace and share that with others through the medium of service.

TEST NUMBER TWO:
SHATTERED PLACES

Transforming despair into hope!

Often times it is the shattered places that house broken people with broken hearts, that empower us to open our souls to the Divine power of the universe. Can it be that we actually find our true selves through the connection of our brokenness to the connection of the broken?

When you are adopting a child, you put yourself into an arena which is understandably impossible for many to understand. One of the constant questions I would get when I was going through an adoption is 'Why don't you just have your own children?' A fair and understandable question, however, my answer would usually surprise people. You see for us adoption was a conscious decision. When I had first moved to Kenya, I would stand at the local bus stop waiting for my 'matatu' to town. The bus stop was next to a rubbish dump and children lived inside it. I knew that to be a good parent you did not have to give birth to the child, and you did not have to share the same blood as the child.

In all my travels I don't think I had encountered such brokenness as that which I found in the orphanage where we adopted

Aaliyah. The brokenness of forty children whose mothers had unsuccessfully attempted to abort them too late in the pregnancy for them to die. Instead, they would live a life in their deformed bodies with oversized heads and undersized arms and legs. They would never walk and possibly never experience the unconditional love of a single human being. They lay helpless on mats on the floor united by the commonality of their histories and present realities.

In my early days in Kenya AIDS was rife and a 'belief' came to the minds of sufferers that they could be cured of their death sentence through intercourse with a child. In the same orphanage I nursed children as young as two whose hearts and lives had been broken into a million pieces through this 'belief'.

Little did I know at the time of Aaliyah's adoption that the shattered places of our past would connect together like the dots in Amalia's colouring books.

In March of 2019 I had gathered a group of friends who had become family together to attend a world music festival held annually in Adelaide. Aaliyah's Godmother and her two children came from interstate and Tashania and her partner came from Melbourne. And together we spent a weekend of fun and laughter, attending the world music festival and many other fringe events including the highlight of the Ethiopian acrobats. It was a warm time of year in Adelaide and being outdoors in the hot summer sun took its toll on all of us. However, the entire weekend Aaliyah was wearing a thinly woven woolen jumper to match her shorts. At one event as we were standing out in the hot sun, I advised Aaliyah to remove her jumper as everyone else was wearing singlet tops, but she refused.

The next morning a dear friend whose daughter had spent the weekend with us called me urgently to say that she had suspicions that Aaliyah was suicidal and was self-harming. My entire body broke out into a cold sweat induced fear. The thoughts that went through my head were incoherent and my children will be the first ones to tell you that I am not the calmest of mothers when it comes to dealing with intense issues.

Once when Tashania was in year 10 at school, a friend had come to me while I was teaching a secondary English class to inform me that Tashania had been so drunk over the weekend that her friends had not been able to get her home from the park they had been drinking in and had actually stolen a rubbish bin and put her inside it to carry her home to bed. While what Tashania did was not anything out of the ordinary for someone her age, my response was to walk down the corridor of the school where she was a student and I was a teacher and literally drag her out of class, pull her into my class-room and give her a very strong piece of my mind with regard to her behaviour.

Now it was Aaliyah and how I was going to respond to this situation could potentially have been a matter of life and death. So, I put the other children to bed, walked into the room where Aaliyah slept and closed the door. I sat down quite calmly and asked her to remove her jumper. She quickly grabbed any part of herself and refused. I remained calm and told her I would not be going anywhere until I had seen her wearing nothing but a singlet top. It did not take her too long to agree and what I saw was a sight no mother should ever have to view. With tears rolling down my cheeks, I looked at my daughters massacred arms. Both arms were completely covered with the marks dug into them with a razor blade.

Aaliyah...my precious Aaliyah (one of great strength and wisdom) had been crippled with pain that she did not know how to express in any other way than to harm her body. The Aaliyah that we had wanted more than anything else in the world, who we fought an entire Kenyan judicial system that was against us. And yet despite what we had done for Aaliyah, I sat there, slumped in my chair feeling like a complete failure as a mother.

As I came back to myself fury set in and I quickly climbed on top of Aaliyah's loft bed to search for anything I could find that in my opinion should not be there. Aaliyah's bed is so high, and she had always refused for anyone, including her younger brother and sister to get onto it. As I removed pillows and blankets, I discovered a red T-shirt completely soaked in the blood of my child and a packet of Panadol's. The fury combined with the shock of the event were now at boiling levels within my being. As has become so common with people my age and their children, the first thing we do in a moment of crisis is blame devices or social media. My usual reaction in events such as these would be to just smash the devices and think that was enough to solve the problems.

Thank Goodness for the entire situation that I had recently done a course in Transcendental Meditation and had become a regular practitioner of this practice of peace. I honestly believe that is what gave me the clarity and insight to handle this situation from a place of grace and dignity and where I believe that I put forward the best version of myself, rather than my previously programmed unconscious worst version of myself.

Through my year of deliberate intention and the work I had been doing on myself, I had already spent a significant amount of my waking hours exploring every possible avenue for repairing my shattered soul. Now I was face to face with the shattered soul of my child.

In a moment of awakening, I heard from a teacher of mine that we are 100% responsible for every person, event, situation, and problem that we draw into our lives. Hmmm! Not and easy concept for many to grasp I must admit, however, I was very lucky. The minute I heard this it seeped into every part of my being, and I just got it. I believe the reason why I got it was because I understood the concept of humans being vibrational beings that operate on vibrational frequencies. I understood that on the level of the soul there is nothing like death. Death is of the body and the soul is eternal. I also understood that the purpose of our soul was to manifest the chosen physical body for the soul purpose of its eternal healing.

With my developing understanding of trauma being a cellular part of our being, I knew that this was something we needed to work on with Aaliyah. After holding my hands in surrender to Aaliyah and telling her I had absolutely no idea how to deal with this, what to say or do, a gifted moment of awakening occurred for the two of us. I talked about fear and love and brought up a topic I had never really thought about before. Aaliyah's conception. Aaliyah and I sat there tenderly and agreed that the probability of her being conceived from a place of love was pretty low. We also agreed that she had probably been conceived through an act of hatred. As I think about it now, I actually wonder which children are in fact conceived out of genuine love. The love of two healed parents who embody the love of self, instead of the marketed version of love towards the other while neglecting and abusing our own soul. I wonder if most of us are in the default mode of love, parenting and having children, the idea of it being so romantic, when the reality of it creates the stuff of nightmares.

That night I did not sleep well. It was like the moment I found out I was terrified about the fact that my daughter may choose not to wake up the next morning. I woke up many times during the night and walked into her room to see if I could hear her breathing. But what about all those nights when I had not been aware of her pain, when I had been so wrapped up in my own that I had not had the energy to even consider if she had been experiencing any.

The next morning, I woke up and called Aaliyah into my bedroom. I sat with her and explained my revised position of the situation. I told her straight up that I could not be held hostage to her threats, even if they were in her own mind, that she may or may not commit suicide. I told her that I would do absolutely everything within my hands to relieve her pain, however I also understood that the pain could be her gift if directed and manifested patiently and without quitting. I told her I didn't believe I was helping her if I pretended, she needed to be alive for me. As her life would continue, she would have to make decisions about jobs, partners, and many other things that I may not agree with, and I explained to her that the same applied to whether she was choosing for her life to remain on this planet or transcend to another. I explained the pain I felt knowing that we wanted her more than anything on earth, but if she decided for herself that it was not our time to be together then I respected that. I also talked about my understanding of the laws of attraction and that the universe divinely orchestrated us being together in this lifetime. We choose each other. As I chose to be her parent, she chose to be my daughter, we were here to heal together.

I explained to Aaliyah that we would use conventional and non-conventional methods to push this journey forward as best we could. I booked her into a Transcendental Meditation course, an energy healing, a psychologist. I respected her wishes not to involve a school counsellor and offered to explore any options she felt may help. But most importantly the first thing I did was book myself into a conscious parenting course. When I told her, this was the first thing I had done she looked at me and said, "but you are a great mother." I responded telling her that if she was in pain, I still had some wounds to heal within myself and that is what I was going to do.

When I first found out about Aaliyahs self-harming, I decided to do some research around what self-harming actually is. In this day and age, we are led to believe that self-harming involves the blade of a razor penetrating the skin enough to draw blood and create scars. This was something that was not any part of my known reality. But what about the socially acceptable self-harming of drawing a nicotine filled stick of tobacco to one's lips and drawing the toxicity into one's lungs, as my father had done his whole life? What about the sugar we as a Western nation consume in quantities out numbering that of cocaine? What about the toxic thoughts that psychically attack our being through media, negativity and the brokenness of ourselves, our systems and those we love? I discovered self-harming is just another opportunity to awaken that which lies inside us unhealed.

In Africa physical scarring through the use of a razor blade that initially draws blood and then leaves intricate designs permanently in the skin is common practice. This is not self-harming. This is a rite of passage. This is a sign of courage, a sign that you have passed through a threshold of life. The scars African warriors carry on their face, arms and legs show that they are alive. That they have felt pain, that their pain has served them in the next phase of their life and that they will move forward stronger, more resilient, more capable than before their scars and with their head held high and dignified.

Within a month of me finding out about Aaliyah's self-harming I had booked my trip to Africa, and I was leaving her in Australia. Some of my friends were absolutely horrified, saying that my biological kids were more important than my adopted kids. I calmly explained to them that Aaliyah had been self-harming in the room next to me and I had had no idea. I knew it was not where I was that was going to prevent or cause that. I knew that leaving Aaliyah after I found out about this was the greatest gift she has ever been given. The gift of Trust. I showed Aaliyah that I trusted her decision either way and that trust was one hundred percent. To this day she lives and breathes the meaning of her name Aaliyah...one of great strength and wisdom.

LIFE HAPPENS THROUGH YOU
AND NOT TO YOU!

A Course in Miracles and Quantum Physics both teach that the world we see outside of ourselves is quite simply a reflection of our internal frame of reference. When I was undergoing narcissistic abuse recovery, I learned and embraced very quickly that there was no part of my abuse that had anything to do with the narcissist. Everything about that situation was a projection of my inner wounds into my external reality. My understanding grew really quickly that life happens through us and not to us, which was also a factor that contributed many years earlier at the beginning of my physical abuse to me denying that I was a victim of it. At that point I was not at all conscious of the so within so without theory, so tended to sit uncomfortably in the place of external woundedness while not really accepting it. In the early and even in the middle stages of my physical, emotional, and financial abuse, my mind had always sat in the 'how can this be happening to me' zone. And from that zone I put myself into a position of defense. I needed to defend my worth as a human, a wife, child, mother, friend, and sister. And needless to say, this generally tended to make the abuse worse. As I was later to learn, there is never a need to defend when you have healed your wounds and know that attack is merely a construct of the mind.

THE DIVINE LAW OF COMPENSATION

"Nothing binds you except your thoughts; nothing limits you except your fears; and nothing controls you except your beliefs." Marianne Williamson. The Divine Law of Compensation.

Marianne Williamson talks regularly of Miracle minded thinking. For me I was very fortunate to have come to the point of my brokenness that the only way was up. I had young children who had a right to a healed mother and the only way for that healing to occur was through a miracle. I had been fortunate enough to see the damage that the projection of my own inner wounds had created onto my children before I had completely screwed all of them up and set them up as receivers of my projected wounds that they would then spend their own lives learning the hard way how to heal.

As I have travelled the world and spent the greater part of my life working in settings dominated by children and as I was fortunate enough to learn from the happenings in my own world. The hardest lesson of all about being a parent came from Dr Shefali where she says the greatest lesson a parent can ever learn about themselves and their children is "No one really truly loves anyone. Everyone loves conditionally. Most love is conditioned, control based, and fear based."

And therein lies the Miracle. The conscious realization of this as a point of truth absolutely changed everything for me. We bring children into this world from a place of pure selfishness. We bring these children to serve as vessels for us to channel our unhealed wounds and project our deficiencies onto. From the moment a child is born we do not love them unconditionally. From day one we place judgments onto those children. Does he/she sleep well, feed well or he/she is a very good baby are very common terminologies and conversations heard around a baby just a few days into this world. We are automatically placing energetic conditions onto that child in the form of conditional love. When we use statements like these what the child learns is that they are only 'good' if they meet a certain set of predefined criteria that quantifies 'good.' And we don't stop doing this when they are babies, these judgments, conditions, and points on our checklists continue throughout a child's life and come out in terms of school grades, sporting accolades, gender, source of income, etc.

Dr Shefali discusses the checklists that we all hold to believe as our personal truths and we project them directly onto our children. Thus, our love is a selfish/ conditioned love and not about the child. We believe if we do not follow the checklist then we are less than. But a child comes into the world as a free spirit. When we place our conditions onto that child what we are really doing is expecting that child to fulfill some unhealed part of ourselves. The child is our mirror, our universal teacher but as we place them into our conditional world governed by fears and limitations what we do to that child has set them up for a world of pain rather than a world of prosperity.

The Divine Law of Compensation forces us to shift the focus of our thinking from the physical plain to the universal one where we learn that miracles are in abundance, mainly because the majority of us have been deflecting them for the greater parts of our lives and they are sitting there waiting to compensate us for this.

As Marianne Williamson states, when we think of ourselves as channels of infinite creative energy of the universe, we think higher thoughts and are lifted to a realm of consciousness where we ask How can I be of service to the world to become more important than what can I get out of this. Within that realm we naturally do get a job, create money, and produce an outer prosperity that reflect our inner prosperity.

This is because the universe is self-organizing and self-correcting. We are meant to be lifted to the highest level of creative possibility in our lives. The Law of divine compensation works on the principles that when we experience diminishment on a physical plain there is a universal level of consciousness that once we open our heart to unconditional love will be downloaded onto our screen and manifested in our reality.

As my year of deliberate intention progressed, we received what to us was the most divine of compensation imaginable. A small windfall that was placed into an account with the soul intention of it being used to make the lives of my children more fulfilling. We were not to know at the time of that deposit the power that divine compensation would have to change the lives of so many.

As we packed our bags in anticipation of this enormous journey we were about to embark on, there was, as with any trip to Africa a lot to prepare. While the intention of this trip was to conduct an on the ground feasibility study for all the research we had undertaken over the previous year (or in reality our whole adult life), the unconscious reality quickly surfaced to the conscious and generated a healing pathway for myself and my children, that to this day continues to grow stronger in its resonance.

We were starting the trip in Qatar, the country of birth for both of my biological children and the country where after living for ten years of my life I was held under country arrest for twelve months. From there we would base ourselves in Kenya, the birthplace of my two adopted children and the fathers of all my kids. Kenya is a main character in the story that is my life and the place where I had stared death in the eye on more than one occasion.

As if that wasn't enough, we would then travel on to Rwanda, with the project team I had gathered together to conduct our feasibility for starting our educational development. Rwanda! Where I had left just three years prior in a state of confusion, wondering exactly what it was I had done wrong. Rwanda! Where some people I had thought to be friends had stopped speaking to me for fear that they may encounter political turbulence due to whatever mystery I had engaged in to have me kicked out so swiftly.

Amalia has seven young cousins in Rwanda, and we were taking gifts for all of them. Arranging for a group of seven isn't easy. I had done most of the shopping and needed to make sure I had similar quantities for everyone. I had taken seven pieces of A4 paper and laid them across my bed. A child's name was written on each piece of paper, and I spent an hour dividing shirts, pyjamas, drink bottles, colouring books, and more into sizes and genders of the children.

With gifts piled up onto the A4 papers on my bed, Amalia came into my room to check out what was happening. She asked me to read the names and as I got to the last name, she said "But mummy, what are we taking for my brothers?" We had not had any contact with Amalia's brothers in Kenya for about two years. During my healing from narcissistic abuse, I had learned about the energetic supply narcissists receive by embedding hatred through their divide and conquer techniques. This is exactly what Mr. Rwanda had done and took great pride in his mastery of this technique. I turned back to Amalia and said "Amalia...I don't think we are going to see your brothers this trip." She turned and looked me straight in the eye and said..." I have to!"

So, I opened my phone, took a deep breath, and sent a message to her oldest brother telling him that we would be coming to Kenya the following week and Amalia would love to see them. I also explained that I completely understood if this was not OK with him or the boy's mother.

Narcissists have this insane capacity to twist and turn genuine relationships as a means of making people feel and doubt their own sanity while filling themselves with narcissistic supply, their drug of choice.

A response came through on my phone almost immediately saying, of course they would love to see us.

Amalia is the embodiment on earth of an angel. She knew within herself the power she had to change her life and the lives of her brothers. The innocence of a child in the cultivation of relationships is something adults can learn from. Children see with their soul. Amalia knew she was going to see her brothers and no amount of politics, adult bickering or narcissistic hatred was going to prevent that from happening.

A week after Amalia had walked into my room and seen the gifts, she was in the loving arms of four of her warriors. Her three brothers in Kenya had met us at the airport when we arrived and along with Marley, we had gone to a beautiful campsite to spend time together before the boys went back to school the following week. As we sat under the African moon, I watched Amalia enveloped by the love of her brothers and was swept away with the feelings of peace and excitement.

A few weeks after arriving in Nairobi we were heading to Rwanda to meet the rest of the In2EdAfrica team and do the feasibility study for our project. Amalia's oldest brother and I had lived together in Rwanda where he had attended university for a year before his father sabotaged his opportunity and convinced him to return to Kenya. As we sat under the African moon on our first night in Kenya, I asked him if he would like to join us in Rwanda. As the evening went on, not only was he coming to Rwanda with us, but he was also going to be part of our start up team, a Director in the Company we were starting and whilst in Rwanda we would fulfill a dream of a lifetime for me and trek Mountain Gorillas.

Driving to the Dianne Fossey Research Centre, through the beauty of this country that we were all connected to, I apologized to my stepson for the fact that he had had to bear witness to the physical, emotional, and financial abuse inflicted upon me by his father. I explained that I was so deeply entrenched in the energetic head fuck of the whole situation that I had not been able to see the truth clearly. There had been times when I had expected him to rescue me and many times that he actually had. During my year of deliberate intention, I apologized to many people who had warned me against this man. I apologized in person to friends in Qatar and Kenya and through other means to people I was not face to face with. Then I stood in the middle of the African jungle, with this young African man, who is a great role model for Amalia and my other children, surrounded by fourteen mountain gorillas and enveloped vulnerability in its purest form.

SOUL CONTRACTS WITH A NARCISSIST

During my year of deliberate intention, I started writing a blog. The title of the blog was nothing is Too Big. I used a uniform picture for every blog post. A concrete statue showing the folded hands of a crossed legged Buddha holding a deep crimson bougainvillea. I poured my heart out every day into these blog posts and wrote what I believed I had learned from every experience I had let into my zone. It was a huge part of exposing my vulnerability to my friends, a lot of whom were very shocked to read some of the details of my life.

I was literally blessed with the realization that the relationship I had with the narcissist was a contract of my soul. I believe wholeheartedly that the narcissist in my life was my soul mate. Not the romantic soul mate that Hallmark and other marketing companies have pioneered us into believing in. I believe that a soul mate is a person who elevates your soul and raises it to its true purpose of being on this earth during this time. Your soul mate is someone with whom you share a soul contract. A contract that has been predetermined through universal forces for the awakening of your soul and shifting it from a place of energetic pain and suffering to one of peace.

I embodied the understanding that our soul actually wants to set us free from the unconscious beliefs and trauma systems that we have, that are in truth the opposite of who we are. The essence of who we are is the light of true divinity. We are powerful, we are peaceful, we are free, however the traumas we have had imprinted on us through our conditioning and patterns of this life and others has not empowered our conscious belief system to understand this. We therefore live in a state that keeps us addicted to trauma, suffering and pain and often times never realize that is how we are living.

A narcissist is a representation of our traumas. They stand in front of us as a mirror to awaken, ignite and heal the internal wounds that prevent us from ever reaching the point of our true purpose on this earth.

I was so fortunate to understand that the narcissist who presented himself into my vortex was in fact and angel in disguise. Sure, there had been other angels before him, but they had never managed the power of the soul connection that was required for me to awaken. They had only gotten so far in the ring and while at the time I was experiencing pain through them, it was not until I experienced the pain of the narcissist that I found the privilege in the awakening that was on the other side of the pain, as I slowly and systematically rose from my knees.

When I understood the gift of narcissistic abuse through the conscious awakening of the higher evolution of the purpose of it, only then was I free to project forward on a journey that was in keeping with the truth of who I am and why I am here. I understood that I had a predetermined soul contract with all the people I drew into my zone. I understood that I was one hundred percent responsible for every one of those people and that I could shift my understanding of my perception through the awareness that life does not actually happen to me.

We are led to believe that life in an external representation. What we see in our outside, physical world is the reality, the truth, the way things are. Absorbing the complete opposite of this ideology is what brought me to an understanding of peace.

PAIN AS MY TEACHER

In my Australian culture, and perhaps others I am not as embedded in, I believe we have been taught to fear pain. We seem to use every chance we get to numb the pain be it physically or emotionally. The reality is pain is not a disease, it is a dis-ease! It is a lack of ease within our body or mind that is telling us it is time to realign!

Through the process of rewriting my script, I have learnt that pain is in fact my teacher. If you make peace with pain and work together to ride the wave, then pain will tell you where you are meant to be next. In fact, as you work with your pain, you find out that it sets you free in a new direction of realignment that you could never have imagined! As energetic beings we are designed to live in a state of flow. Pain is a blockage of the flow of energy that is our truth. I don't believe that medicating that pain is of service to our soul, as the medication suppresses the pain and prevents the flow of our lifeforce energy.

However, working with pain is not easy, because you have to look within yourself. We have been socially and culturally conditioned to look outside of ourselves for answers. We look to others to solve our pain, doctors, partners, teachers, lawyers, medications, anything that deflects us from facing the truth and looking within. When transitioning from a fear of pain towards a love of it, you have to be brutally honest with yourself and you have to rip off all those internal band aids you have unconsciously positioned since you were a child. You have to expose those wounds before you can heal them. And trust me, those wounds are grotesque. Mine were overflowing with puss, toxicity, infection, and darkness. But what was my choice really? To continue living with all that crap inside my energetic being, or to rip them open, see them as the battle scars that had made me into a warrior, heal them and move forward with pain as my teacher and peace in my heart.

The pain of losing my children became a valuable lesson for me. Over time I began to understand that pain is not pain in and of itself. Pain is a by-product of thought. Because I thought my children were meant to live side by side with me throughout their childhood that thought was what caused me to feel the pain. Pain is connected to a judgment. Again, my personal judgment and the judgment of others was in many cases, the actual cause of the emotion I was calling pain.

A simple shift in that judgment meant I could shift the feeling from one of pain to one of joy. And this is when the pain became my teacher. The pain I felt over the 'loss' of my children has become the greatest source of my joy. Not one day goes by now where I am not grateful for every moment, I spend with them. The lives that we live together now are lives that are full of peace, contentment and joy and the simple reason for that is pain. The reality of pain is that it is just a perception. Pain is not real; it is the result of a thought and the energy we channel into maintaining the thinking in the manner that continues to create pain. Once we choose to heal, pain disappears.

When I became aware of pain as a tool, as a teacher and as the source of healing, then I was on my way to being free of it! Where I feel I have been caused enormous amounts of pain from people, their perception may be that they have done nothing wrong. Thus, pain lies in the beliefs that we believe are realities but which in actual fact are illusions. The greater the pain the harder the lesson and the bigger the transformation. The bigger the transformation, the greater the gratitude for the pain. And so, you become aligned! It is then that you understand that pain is simply an avenue to lead your spirit to uncovering the truth of who you really are.

In essence, the outside world is a projection of our inner wounds.

TEST NUMBER 3

"We are never upset for the reason that we think" ACIM

As my year of deliberate intention started nearing the end of its calendar stage, the intention of that year was beginning to morph more into a life of deliberate intention. I had learned so much about myself and my priorities that I felt moving forward with a life of deliberate intention was going to be something that would benefit myself and those around me.

In August of 2019, I received a call from our construction engineer who was based on the ground in Kenya saying construction of the first school was completed and that people in the local community were keen to enroll their children and get started. Being September, this meant that students would only be in our facility for one term before the academic year came to an end and as an educator it surprised me that parents would be so eager to move their children from one school to another at this point of the academic year. Despite my reservations, my teammate led me to believe it was very important for me to return to Kenya, to train the teachers and set up the school for a September opening, along with being there to oversee start up developments of our second school. Mum agreed to stay with the children as this was to be a short trip and by September I was back in Nairobi.

I rented an apartment in Nairobi and three of my teammates stayed together. We were fully resourcing one school, planning the construction of the second and organizing government and company registrations, so there was a lot to do in just two weeks. My days were filled with meetings, networking and organizing matters. In the mornings, the team and I will sit down over coffee and decide upon the tasks required to be completed that day. Then we would head off in various directions and possibly meet back in the evening or possibly not. In the morning I was told how much money was needed for the days tasks and I would hand it over trustingly...big mistake! As deadlines were being missed and accountability was being sought by me in the form of receipts of payments and documentation to support government required paperwork, I asked our construction engineer many times, only to be given excuse after excuse.

I was on a really strict timeline as my kids were back in Australia and I needed to get home. As the knock-on effects of incompletion of tasks started interfering with other jobs, I put the guy to whom I had given a large amount of money to build the school on the spot. In that instant he went head-spinningly crazy over the phone, ranting and raving at me for twenty long minutes. With the phone on speaker (and record), my two friends and I who bore witness to the insanity knew this was not going to end well. The next day he came back into the apartment while the rest of us were out, collected his things and disappeared with the money and an incomplete job.

This is a situation I had played out on numerous occasions in this lifetime, however now the canvas it was playing out on was not a water colour. This paint was bold and striking, it knew

302

what could and couldn't be diluted on or through the canvas. This time, I knew so well that anywhere there is anger, pain or a feeling of upset is in fact a set up. I was being set up through this test of my healing. I was being tested to see if any of the wounds had not fully healed. To see if there was still some puss remaining that needed to be cleared. I was being set up to see if I would fall into my old perceptions of thought and default actions. I was being set up to see if blame would raise its head. Would my sense of worth be violated, or would the uncomfortable comfort of my fetal position resurface?

And as his words came firing like the venom of a spitting cobra towards me, ready to infiltrate my being with their toxic intention, I did not get angry. I remained calm. I did not raise my voice as a response to his poison. I did not hang up the phone as a response to his insanity. I did not feel upset, nor did I feel even a speck of pain as his anger rose and his abusive language, tone and demeanor heightened.

I had had enough of the suffering caused by people like him towards people like me. In that moment I knew I had awakened to the fact that I had a choice to go beyond what I perceived as being wrong and remain in a state of love for what is real and true. If I had taken his attack personally, he would not have suffered any more than he already was, it would have been me who would have bought into that pain and suffering and inflicted it upon myself.

And so, while my teammates were understandably horrified at this behaviour, I sat in a space of gratitude. The exquisite beauty of this set up had not upset me. I took responsibility for the fact that I had drawn both this person and this experience into my zone and both of them had been angels in my journey of healing. This man was an incarnation of Mr. Rwanda. What he said and did was parallel to what I had been through at the hands of the narcissist. The huge difference here was my response. Through all of the insanity and the loss of a huge amount of money, I felt so proud of myself because I had responded from a place of what I believed to be in that moment as grace. I had not shown the worst version of myself as I had done for years at the hand of the narcissist, this time was different. This time I was standing tall, surrounded by integrity and an energy of light filled resilience that I knew was going to make our project stand from the same field as we moved forward into the future.

It is in and through the silence that the answers are to be found.

As my year of deliberate intention was coming to an end, the year itself had both transformed and was transforming. The creation of that year had shaped the rewriting of the script I would take with me as I moved forward. No longer would I be caught in the drama and addiction of the past. The psychic attacks on my being no longer had the capacity to connect with the truth of who I was. Sure, the tests of my healing would still come and go, but I was now conscious of how I could and would respond to them. Rather than becoming the victim of them, I would become the grateful receiver of them.

When I first moved back to Australia, I had made the decision that I was not moving home, I had tried that twenty years before, and it had not worked. This time I had my head around the fact that I was moving on to another experience. If I could manoeuvre the worlds and systems inside countries like Qatar, Kenya, and Rwanda, then surely, I could do the same thing in Australia where I had some understanding of the people, language, and systems. As I had done in every country I had lived in, I became the observer. And what I observed in Australia was shocking. I found people everywhere running on a hamster wheel. Men, women, and children who had all bought into the systemic conditioning of consumerism. People who believed fully in the fact that two parents 'had' to work in order to create the lifestyle that they 'enjoyed.' So, their children could have the 'life' they deserved. And through my observations what I was seeing was parents who found little joy in their work or their children, or the house they were pumping so much time and money into. Children who were over programmed by parents who were caught in the false safety of the busyness trap. Hundreds if not thousands of people who were unconsciously running on a hamster wheel and getting absolutely nowhere. People who were so energetically addicted to the pain and suffering caused by buying into the collective paradigm of happiness, success, and life that as they ran on the wheel like a hamster, life was passing them by and before they knew it, they would be struck down by an awakening and then be in the same position I had been in. Choose to live or die. The hamster wheel does not give anyone the opportunity to live. On that wheel you run and run and run and the slow death of that style of running leads to nowhere other than the grave.

What the world didn't want us to know is that the answers are not found on the wheel. The answers to life are found when we become still. During my year of deliberate intention, I became still. The busy life I had led was stripped away, my self- and society-imposed belief of identity was stripped away. I was still. The stillness initially came through the form of yoga and meditation, however as the year morphed, the stillness became a constant presence no matter what I was doing, where I was or who I was with. Through the stillness I found all the answers about who I was, what I was here for and most importantly exactly what my future would look like. It was through the stillness that I was in a position to access the place of all knowing. I had been conditioned to believe that place resided outside of me. In a university, in a partner, a job, my kids. There is nothing like that. The place of all-knowing lies deep within my soul. The reason why I had never found it was because I had never remained still for long enough. The longer the stillness, the louder the voice became.

There are people who find the stillness but along with it they also ignite the fear of staying there. When you find the stillness, you lose other things. People, places, memories, beliefs, ideologies, values and for some, that loss is too painful to consciously work through, so the default hamster wheel kicks back in and cranks its cogs even faster.

I have been raised in a culture that values talk over silence. I am in environments where people find silence deafening. Where they believe that the essential joys of life are found through the noise of the television, a football match, the screaming of a child or spouse. While these events may create enjoyment when applied consciously to one's existence, when they are unconscious, they simply feed the addiction to suffering because they deflect the essence of silence and thus prevent the surfacing of all knowledge.

Often our socially conditioned paradigms are in conflict with the choice to be quiet. Many have never really questioned the whole hamster wheel scenario, how it came about and who it actually serves. We don't question the noise; we think it is normal. For me, the noise was noisy. It was painful and constricting, it was stopping me, but I didn't know it at the time. The noise was a part of the energetic prison that had enveloped me and kept me trapped like the bars of a prison cell. The noise hid the knowledge, the wisdom, and the truth. This is why so many people find meditation such a transformative process. As we train ourselves to be still, to be silent, the truth starts shining, from a tiny spark to an inferno. Through the silence comes a release that will change who you are forever. As you are still the barricades will fall. One by one, the barricades of guilt, shame, worthlessness, betrayal, fear, dishonesty will fall. In the silence as they fall, they are replaced. Through the stillness, the true purpose of our being manifests through the form of a commitment to peace which will walk forward with you even in the noisiest of environments.

CONSCIOUS EDUCATION

Khalil Gibran in The Prophet tells of children. Here we learn: "Your children are not your children. They are the sons and daughters of life's longing for itself."

After a school trip with Marley's grade three class, I had the courage to offer my services to the teacher in the capacity of listening to children read. I said I would come into her class 3 mornings a week and volunteer. Two books in and I knew I had a little more to offer than a mum listening to reading. I proposed some intensive intervention groups on phonics and math's for groups of children to boost them. I was a registered and qualified teacher after all and for the teacher to get this service free of charge for three mornings a week, she was nothing short of amazed.

Spending time as an observer in the classroom created some major awakenings for me. Marley went to a great school. The teachers are amazing and the leadership second to none. And yet a lot of what I was seeing, and feeling was a discontentment with the students, including my own child. Children started opening up to me, telling me stories of mum never being around, or dads who had left for reasons from death, to divorce or even fuelling their addiction to working. The classroom was a collective energetic pool of broken children who were sometimes making it through the day in one piece and sometimes not. When I had first moved to Adelaide a friend had told me that her goal for her child who was just about to start secondary school was for her to survive. I had been shocked. Surely survival was a given and the goal for our children's educational journey would be more connected to them gaining a holistic foundation for them to take forward into life with them.

So, I reflected on the fact that I had spent twenty-five years educating other people's children and perhaps now was the time for me to make that investment into my own. Amalia was just completing kindergarten and Marley was about to finish Grade Three. I had already met some mums who were home-schooling through the trampolining club the kids went to. One mum had four children ranging from university level to kindergarten and one of the most notable things about her children were how kind they were to each other. The older children were very kind to the younger ones, and it was so refreshing to see in a place where previously I had seen children and siblings in particular in a war against themselves and each other.

I contacted the home-schooling branch of the South Australian education department, made the decision, filled the forms and we were good to go. The first part of home-schooling in our case was really about changing Marley's self-esteem from that of believing that he was stupid to believing that he was unstoppable. We were no longer governed by early morning wake ups which meant we were also not as governed by get to bed by a particular time. One of the things I had loved about having a live-in house maid when my children were little and I was a working mother was the fact that even though I had to get up in the morning, they didn't. They were never dropped anywhere.

They never had to get up in the morning even as babies and I really believe this removed huge amounts of stress from their early years. I had tried the drop and go method many years earlier when I had returned to Australia with Tashania. It made our mornings very stressful, constricted our lifestyle and was one of the variables high on my list for eventually deciding to leave Australia again and create a life in a country where I had the option of live in-house help.

PSYCHOLOGIST

My psychologist told me I needed to find like-minded people! While she was right to a certain extent, what I also needed was a paper trail. I was not a fan of paper trails. I didn't keep receipts and loved the feeling of channeling the energy of paper from my being into the rubbish bin. However, this was Australia. I learned very quickly that the paper trail can make or break your case, no matter what the case is.

Being back in Australia, I had to learn how to do things the Australian way. The difficult part was that many people who had been in Australia all their lives were not even consciously aware of what the Australian way was. So, I was learning and teaching at the same time. Neither of which was always as well received as it was intended. When you live outside your culture is when you actually discover what your culture is. When you remain inside it you believe there is a 'normal.' Normal way of behaving, speaking, socializing, common sense. However, the minute you step outside of your 'normal' is when you discover that there actually isn't a 'normal.'

I had met three lawyers in Australia regarding custody and they had all literally done my head in, so the psychologist was a good balance. So, I talked, and she wrote. I talked once a fortnight for about a year and she created a file. At the end I decided I had talked enough, and I felt she had written enough. I am so grateful that until now we have never had to use her notes.

HEAVEN AND HELL- MANIFESTING THE COOLEST LIFE OR THE PERFECT NIGHTMARE

When I had been lying on the floor, energetically paralyzed, barely able to crawl from one place to another, I understood I had two choices. I could continue to live in the hell that I had created for myself, or I could choose to create my version of heaven. In our goal orientated society, we are taught that heaven is something that we work towards, something that is in the future, that we must work hard to obtain. In actual fact we are taught that heaven is something we have to die for in order to find. This version creates so much pain as it is the complete opposite of present moment. I understood that if I was going to manifest the coolest life that I had to think differently, otherwise what I had and was doing was creating the perfect nightmare for myself and my children. Heaven is found in the present moment; peace is found in the present moment. Heaven is a choice of our thoughts, and I believe that with conscious intention we can find the essence that is heaven in every moment of our lives despite external circumstances that are occurring around us.

In2EdAfrica has become the manifestation of the coolest possible life for me at the moment. It blossomed as a result of the work I put into myself and has enabled the epicentre for transformational change. I believe working on yourself takes courage. You have to be ready to face your demons head on, to rewrite the pre-programmed script that has been placed upon you from your birth and take 100% responsibility for everything that has and will happen in your life. There can be no more deflecting of the self by busying yourself. That is just deflecting from your truth. When I think about the coolest possible life, I would have could manifested for myself, my children, and the people around me, it is exactly the life I have created. My children have every right to be given the gift of a healed mother. A mother who puts herself first, rather than abandoning herself for the needs of others.

So, I wonder now, if you as the reader can see the essence of everything I have written through the quote at the beginning of the book that I believe is worth repeating...

"Our deepest fear is not that we are inadequate.

Our deepest fear is that we are powerful beyond measure.

We ask ourselves

Who am I to be brilliant, gorgeous, talented, fabulous?

Actually, who are you not to be?

We were born to make manifest the Glory of God that is written within us.

And as we let our own light shine, we unconsciously give other people permission to do the same..."

PART THREE
REALIZATION OF MY PURPOSE

IN2ED AFRICA IS BORN

"Where there is love there is no darkness." African Proverb

Birthing a new way forward.

I came to the understanding in my late 40's and as I went through my narcissistic abuse recovery program that everything that had occurred in my life before that date was a part of my evolutionary process where I needed to put together all the parts of myself that led me to a full conscious understanding of what my purpose was.

In order to follow the inner force of my true self I needed to understand the inner journey of knowing the power of choice I had in the expression of myself. What I began to understand was that I had negotiated my power through forces outside myself. And where I had given the perception to others that I was confident etc, on the inside my self-esteem was in a state of chaos.

What I needed was a sense of meaning and purpose. From the bottom of my soul, I needed to know what the power of my soul was, what the power of my mind was and how this was going to translate into the experience of myself. So, I expanded my reality and tried new things that changed me. I expanded my interior, and in making those choices profound consequences were unlocked and expanded. I learned that through the experience of my inner self an appetite to find my highest potential became a burning desire. And this burning desire was a desire of my soul. I had managed to make peace with my ego and connect with the purpose of my soul where from the deepest part of my being there was no other option. This was not something I could choose; it is something that was chosen for me from the time I entered this realm. No matter how many times I had deviated from it in my life, it was there and there was no choice. It was the truth of who I am. And there my highest potential was born.

I realized that reaching my highest potential came from that which I must cope with and not that which I was necessarily choosing to do. But my highest potential was not what I do it was who I became...the truth of who I am.

I spent a year researching various educational developments in Africa. I looked at programs that were deemed 'successful' and I looked at programs that had gone under. I examined the politics behind the programs and how politics also became a player in the demise or success of various programs. With all my experience in Africa I knew that charity was not something I was interested in expanding. I knew that I wanted to be a part of something transformative and something that would have collaboration as its core value. From my experience in Africa and having moved back to the West, I knew that the wealth that Africa had to offer the West was equal if not greater than the wealth the West had to offer Africa. So, I needed to research this concept and connect it to the vision of how we could transform global landscapes through the medium of education.

Since my early days in Kenya, I had experimented with a multitude of different business options. I had started by sending African necklaces that I would buy from the Maasai Market on Globe Cinema roundabout. I would spend hours at the post office on Harambee Ave in the days when we used air mail letters and had to put stamps on envelopes and send the parcels to my mum in Australia who would sell them through various stores in Adelaide. The money from these necklaces would pay my rent and support my lifestyle in Nairobi until I landed my first job there.

When I first returned to Australia when Tashania was two years old, I set up the first African hair extension import business, where I connected with the hair supplier in Nairobi, balanced the weight of heavy handicrafts and shoes with the light weight of the hair extensions and had them shipped to Australia where we started a successful business in both hair extensions and handicrafts. After leaving Australia and heading to Malaysia when Tashania was four, I started importing African Maasai beaded sandals and ethnic style handicrafts to Malaysia where they were stocked in a lot of the hotel gift shops down the East Coast of Malaysia to cater to the tourist market and filling the gap of locally crafted souvenirs.

When I moved to Qatar, my business options grew in size and scale. The first one involved purchasing a Toyota land Cruiser from the second-hand car market in Dubai and having it shipped to Nairobi where it would later and after much drama be sold. Deciding not to continue with the car idea, we shifted into the concept of exporting Mangos from Mombasa in Kenya to Qatar. This was done through connections we had in farming in Mombasa and an Iranian man based in Qatar who was the owner of the country's largest fruit and vegetable import company in the country.

At the same time, I opened a pair of day spas in Nairobi Kenya, while I was still working as a teacher in Qatar. The idea of the spas was to create a transformative experience for women through the concept of self-care. I had met a massage therapist on one of my trips who gave me the best massage I had ever had. She had been working in a five-star hotel in Mombasa and had recently relocated to Nairobi. We employed her, exported the fittings and fixtures from Dubai and were good to go. What I hadn't realised at the time was that it was a common school of thought in Nairobi and particularly in areas that were predominantly low income that men were to be the main customers of our services and they were not looking for the same sort of massage that I was used to receiving. These men were expecting to receive a 'happy ending' and this was most certainly not a part of our offerings. Mind you we would probably have turned over a higher revenue and not had to shut our doors while staying true to our values.

As I ran the spas, I was also running a recruitment business where I set up an office in Nairobi and started bringing Kenyan ladies to Qatar to work as domestic house helps. After a short disastrous stint of doing this through a Qatar recruitment agent who brought ladies to work in local households, I decided to go out on my own and bring ladies to work for friends and teachers who I worked with. I would travel to Nairobi every six weeks to interview ladies. Most were single parents who would leave their children with their own mothers in Kenya while they set off abroad seeking a steady income and the opportunity to provide greater security for their children. In between this I would interview clients in Qatar who were taking the leap of bringing someone from a foreign country to live in their houses in Qatar, and be responsible for these ladies. It was a huge decision for many people and the logistics were enormous. I would arrange the visa processing, air tickets and all logistics, but I was also responsible for settling ladies into their respective families and teaching them how to behave in the capacity of a housemaid. Most ladies were professionally qualified and found they would earn more money as a housemaid in Qatar than they would as a professional in Kenya if they had the opportunity to get a job in Kenya. Kenyans started flooding into Qatar to work in various employment sections and many found it difficult to conform with the strict rules that Qatar had, including no drinking of alcohol permitted and no sex outside of marriage. Pregnancy outside of marriage was punishable with seven years in jail and as ladies started getting pregnant and crimes including drinking and sex were on the rise, the Qatari government ruled that they would stop giving visas to Kenyans for some time. Having brought about one hundred ladies into Qatar, the business was now wrapped up and I was very pleased to be out of it all.

It took me a long time to learn the simple concept of, if you are running operations in Kenya or Africa the easiest way to do that is to do it in the field that you are familiar with in your own country. Sounds simple enough, but that was a twenty-year learning journey for me.

And so, we came full circle, back to what we do best, which is education and more specifically outside the box education that does not simply buy into the regulated model of a school or what education looks like. We would be more than another 'mzungu' fitting into the cliché of I have a school in Africa. We would be an educational development that was specifically designed to provide high quality education through sustainable models of development to people in resource poor communities.

Through the process of my research, I also started talking to various people about the concept I was brewing. I really wanted to start in Rwanda, and I really wanted a team of people who shared the vision but had their own skill set that they would bring to the project.

In May of 2019 I drew together a team of people from around the world of which the only thing they had in common was that they all knew me. Dan and I had become friends in Qatar where he had been working as an engineer on the construction of the new Doha airport. He was based in Mombasa and would fly with us through Nairobi to Kigali for our feasibility study. Emma my long-term friend and I had met in Kenya when she was on her first teaching post out of university. She was based in the UK and would also join us for our feasibility study of Kenya and Rwanda in May of 2019. Paul was based in Kigali, Rwanda and was a much-respected educationalist based in one of the international schools in Kigali. We had met when I was acting principal of that school and I knew he would be a valuable member of the grounds staff team in Rwanda. It wasn't until I had arrived in Nairobi and Amalia had instigated the reconnection with her brothers that Nester would become part of the team. He was to bring the wisdom of youth, an incredible understanding of Nairobi and Kenya that although he was one, came from the place of observer. He and I were also somewhat kindred souls and had a unity in the abuse that we had both seen and experienced at the hands of his father.

On the 11th of May 2019 we all boarded a plane from Nairobi to Kigali. Emma had flown into Nairobi a few days before and Dan the day before and along with Marley, Nester and Amalia I was so excited to be showing all these people how incredible Rwanda is.

In Kigali we rode motorcycles to meet lawyers, walked up hills to attend meetings, drove out of town to look at schools, talked to teachers and former teachers, principals, and former principals, met with government officials and anyone else who we could find to discuss the concept of our project. As time went by, we discovered our very small start-up budget would not meet the Rwandan standards of building and construction. On the day before Emma and Dan were to leave, we sat around our huge kitchen table in the Airbnb we had rented, examining all the information we had gathered through our feasibility of starting up in Rwanda and decided at that point in time it was not going to work with us.

With the realization that the start-up budget was not going to cut it, I suggested to the team that we start in Kenya on a piece of land that I already owned in Kenya, just out of Nairobi. I had thought we could make a simple structure that would serve initially to secure some further funding that we could use to expand our operations. Almost immediately the decision was made, and this was going to be the simplest way to move operations forward in a timely manner. The next step was to register the name and get things moving.

I had already decided on the name Think Global Academies. A lot of thought had gone into this name well before any of us had boarded a plane to Africa. I had researched that Academies hold a psychological advantage when it comes to naming a school (I can't remember the rationale behind this). Think Global was exactly what I wanted for the students in our school and the people working with our project. We were creating a model of education that was going to embrace thinking globally and as mentioned earlier was going to be more than just a school.

Our application to apply for the registration of our company under the name Think Global Academies was rejected. We had literally already printed the T shirts and I was so shocked to find out that this was not going to be the name we would use.

We had to go back to the drawing board, and it was not as easy as one might think to come up with the name that was going to serve the Brand and the organization as close to perfection as possible.

After what felt like forever, with more lists and brainstorming that we care to remember I was sitting in my friend's house in Nairobi flicking through the pages of a magazine when a page opened with a cargo ship carrying huge containers. It had something written on the side, which I can't even remember but made me think of the band U2. The number 2 resonated with me, and I started playing with combinations, when In2Ed-Africa flowed from my hand onto the page. After that Nester and I made a whole set of possible combinations for the name. We are In2 education in Africa. We are In2 sustainable education etc and so the name was born. Again, with many failed attempts to register, we had to use In2EdAfrica as our trading name and have a separate company name. Now we really were ready to print the T-Shirts!

The children and I left Kenya at the end of May 2019. Construction was well underway on the building of our first school and excitement was everywhere. On the day before we left, we had lunch with Amalia's uncle. He had been asking to meet me frequently during our visit and while we had met once, we had not paid a visit to his property inside the ghetto that he had really wanted me to see. I think subconsciously I knew this property was going to fulfill the dream I had created of building schools in low-income communities and providing high quality education within these facilities. However consciously I knew that I did not want to relive any of the past drama that had been created through my relationship with Mr. Rwanda and Amalia's uncle was his brother.

It was a warm Nairobi day and as we sat eating lunch, the topic of conversation was his property in the ghetto and how we really needed to see it. Within the hour we were in an Uber heading to Korogocho. I had been there before and always loved the vibrancy and excitement inside the ghetto, but this day was different. As we walked in between the corrugated metal sheets that were roughly positioned together to provide local residents with shelter, I knew this was going to be our next school.

We balanced on uneven wooden stairs that stood like a ladder up to the first floor. Maneuvered across planks that served as flooring across the upper floors and felt the anticipation of the bright brown eyes peering from behind thin metal sheets that acted as doors. The recently paved roads in the ghetto were already creating massive transformation as was the development of a huge hospital not far from where our school would be. The paved roads gave Marley and Amalia an opportunity to show off their scooters and scooter skills to the hundreds of children who had gathered around them to enjoy some difference to their day.

I knew this was just what we needed as part of our development, however there was also a huge element of unhealed fear that I could not shake. My year of deliberate intention had provided me with so much growth and healing, that I did not want anything to get in the way of me maintaining that sense of peace. We particularly did not want Mr Rwanda to have anything to do with potentially sabotaging all the hard work we were putting into our healing.

Back in town and sitting outside Charlie's Café opposite the High Court's, whose corridors I had frequented during my two adoptions many years before, I talked openly to Amalia's uncle about his desire to transform this space into a school. I expressed my fears as well as my excitement as did he. And as we balanced ourselves on the plant pots outside the café it was decided that this would be the location for our second development. The next day the children and I left Nairobi and headed back to Australia. We had been away for six weeks and in that time, we had been to three countries. Healed fractured relationships, started the construction of two educational facilities in Kenya, planned to be back in Kenya that same December to prepare the openings of the schools and head back to Rwanda to conduct teacher training and build a library.

As In2EdAfrica started manifesting into the reality that it was to become, I too manifested what I believe is the essence of life. I stepped into a world of infinite possibility that had the capacity to dream the world into being. I came to understand that through my process of healing, I put myself into the position of developing a sustainable future for myself and others. I no longer needed to fill a hole within me with stuff, things, drama, adventure, or anything other than the intention to be of service. For it is when we are of service to others that we are of service to ourselves. This cellular understanding that started to manifest in my being was the opposite of anything I had ever been raised to believe about life and this is where miracles lie.

I transformed my wounds into sources of compassion and generosity. The wounds that had been so painful for me were now consciously at the surface of awareness and created in me an understanding of oneness. My pain is the collective pain and vice versa. As I emptied my heart of the wounds, they were replaced with the capacity to be of service and in service and therein lies the birth of In2EdAfrica.

In2EdAfrica is not a school in Kenya. I drive my team crazy by constantly telling them that we are not a school, we are a brand. But what is that brand? For me, the brand that In2EdAfrica embodies is that of a transformative process where we show it is possible to use the pain and woundedness of our past to create a platform of opportunity, oneness, collaboration, and inspiration. In2EdAfrica is the physical manifestation of my shattered pieces that have been healed with threads of gold and come back stronger, wiser, more compassionate and with the capacity to find joy in every moment of every day in the middle of every process. And therein lies the Miracle.

One of the most beautiful processes about the sacred healing of life, is that as I have transformed myself from a wounded position to one of purpose, what I have done is given my children, the children of my teammates and the children we work with, the permission to stand in their truth. For when we stand in our truth and our children stand in theirs the essence of light shines across the world and it is only then that peace is permanent.

I have come to embody with every core of my being the difference between fate and destiny. As I look back on the pages of this book, I see that while nothing was too big in part one, what I would now define that as is my fate. The sacred healing of life however is my destiny. When I made the shift from fate to destiny and summoned the spirit of my truth then destiny manifested all around. My destiny did not come while I sat and waited. It didn't come while I travelled and moved and engaged in toxic relationships. Sure, those elements of my life were all parts that contributed to my whole, but my destiny came through the discovery of my true purpose. My reason for being on this planet at this time. I really believe that our truth is never about the destination, it is about our destiny. Our destiny is when we understand that we are co-creators of all the beauty and wonder that life has to offer us. Destiny is our truth of purpose. This is our birth right. But it is not our right unless we put in the work and accept one hundred percent responsibility for all the people, places, and situations we draw into our zone. When we fully embody gratitude and eliminate any low frequency vibration that keeps us addicted but never serves our destiny. Destiny is not our fate it is the truth of who we are as whole, spiritual beings. Destiny is crafted by the self. In my experience destiny is embodied when we understand the physical limitations, we buy into that position us towards a life driven by fate and replace them with the pure beauty and innocence of the soul.

"Every human thought, word, or deed is based on fear or love. Fear is the energy which contracts, closes down, draws in, hides, hoards, harms. Love is the energy which expands, opens up, sends out, reveals, shares, heals. You have free choice about which of these to select." Neil Donald Walsh

Nothing Is Too Big
ISBN: 978-4-82414-316-7

Published by
Next Chapter
2-5-6 SANNO
SANNO BRIDGE
143-0023 Ota-Ku, Tokyo
+818035793528

29th April 2022